SCHOLASTIC

BOOK OF WORLD RECORDS ULTIMATE QUIZ CHALLENGE

BY JENIFER CORR MORSE
A GEORGIAN BAY BOOK

SCHOLASTIC REFERENCE
An Imprint of
SCHOLASTIC

Created and produced by Georgian Bay Associates, LLC

Copyright © 2008 by Georgian Bay Associates. All rights reserved.
Published by Scholastic Inc., *Publishers since 1920.*

Georgian Bay Staff
Bruce S. Glassman, Executive Editor
Jenifer Corr Morse, Photo Editor
Amy Stirnkorb, Design

Scholastic Reference Staff
Mary Varilla Jones, Senior Editor
Brenda Murray, Associate Editor
Lucas Klauss, Intern
Becky Terhune, Art Director

ISBN 10: 0-439-88971-5
ISBN 13: 978-0-439-88971-1

10 9 8 7 6 5 4 3   08 09 10 11
Printed in the U.S.A.   23
First printing, January 2008

CONTENTS

1

How many honeybees does it take to produce one teaspoon of honey?

A. 3
B. 12
C. 25

2

How many slices of pizza are consumed each second in the United States?

A. 35
B. 110
C. 350

3

How many kernels of corn are on a cob?

A. 325
B. 650
C. 800

4

How many glasses of milk can one cow produce in a year?

A. 12,000 **B.** 35,000 **C.** 51,000

5

What is the most popular pizza topping in Japan?

A. Seaweed
B. Squid
C. Mango

6

How many eggs are produced in the United States each year?

A. 28 billion
B. 87 billion
C. 140 billion

FOOD

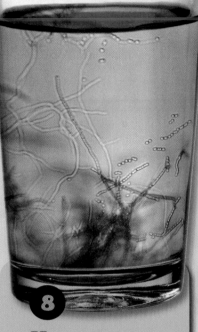

7

How many pounds of food does the average person eat per year?

A. 500 pounds
B. 1,000 pounds
C. 1,500 pounds

8

How many bacteria are in one liter of drinking water?

A. 50,000
B. 100,000
C. 400,000

9

Which holiday has the highest candy sales?

A. Halloween
B. Easter
C. Valentine's Day

What U.S. city eats the most hot dogs?

A. New York City, NY
B. Los Angeles, CA
C. Detroit, MI

What is the most popular type of chocolate in the United States?

A. Dark chocolate
B. Milk chocolate
C. White chocolate

What state produces the most ice cream?

A. Wisconsin
B. Michigan
C. California

FOOD

13

How many conversation hearts are produced for Valentine's Day each year?

A. 1 billion
B. 8 billion
C. 15 billion

14

How many cherries are on an average cherry tree?

A. 1,000
B. 3,500
C. 7,000

15

How much dry pasta is sold each year in the United States?

A. 100,000 pounds
B. 600,000 pounds
C. 1.3 million pounds

16

How many peanuts does it take to make a jar of peanut butter?

A. 200
B. 850
C. 1,400

17

How many types of rice are grown worldwide?

A. 12,000
B. 25,000
C. 40,000

18

What country drinks the most soda?

A. Mexico
B. Australia
C. United States

FOOD

19

What country produces the most fruit?

A. Brazil
B. Argentina
C. China

20

What country has the most fast-food restaurants?

A. China
B. United States
C. Australia

21

What is the world's largest food franchise?

A. Subway
B. McDonald's
C. Dunkin' Donuts

22

How many seeds are on the average strawberry?

A. 50
B. 100
C. 200

23

What is the most popular fruit in the United States?

A. Banana
B. Orange
C. Apple

24

How much milk does it take to make 1 pound of cheese?

A. 0.25 gallons
B. 1.25 gallons
C. 5.25 gallons

FOOD

25

What was the original name of Pepsi?

A. Cold Chill
B. Brad's Drink
C. Pep Cola

26

What's the top-selling hamburger day in the United States?

A. Saturday
B. Sunday
C. Friday

27

What is the most popular flavor of ice cream?

A. Chocolate
B. Vanilla
C. Strawberry

 28

How many lollipops can one lollipop machine make per minute?

A. 5,900
B. 7,000
C. 8,300

 29

Who sells the most fresh-grilled hot dogs?

A. 7-Eleven
B. Street vendors
C. Nathan's

 30

How many doughnuts does Krispy Kreme produce daily?

A. 1.0 million
B. 3.0 million
C. 7.5 million

FOOD

31

How many bowls of cereal does the average American eat annually?

A. 35
B. 100
C. 160

32

How many Oreos would it take to equal the span of the Golden Gate Bridge?

A. 10,400
B. 28,800
C. 45,750

33

How many cans of soda does it take to fill an Olympic-sized swimming pool?

A. 0.6 million
B. 2.7 million
C. 5.5 million

34

How many boxes of Barnum's Animal Crackers would it take to equal the weight of an African elephant?

A. 18,725
B. 30,160
C. 60,235

36

How many hot dogs will Americans consume at ballparks during the summer?

A. 5.5 million
B. 27.5 million
C. 41.3 million

35

How many teaspoons of sugar are in a 12-ounce can of soda?

A. 3
B. 9
C. 16

38

What is the most popular food to cook on the grill?

A. Steak
B. Hamburgers
C. Chicken

37

How many heart-shaped boxes of candy are sold in the United States each Valentine's Day?

A. 13 million
B. 36 million
C. 60 million

39

How many licks does it take for a kid to finish a single scoop of ice cream?

A. 22
B. 50
C. 77

40

Popcorn is the official snack food of what state?

A. Alabama
B. Kansas
C. Illinois

41

On average, how many bags of peanuts does an airline serve each year?

A. 68 million bags
B. 93 million bags
C. 135 million bags

42

How many pounds of French fries does Walt Disney World sell each year?

A. 1 million
B. 9 million
C. 17 million

SPORTS

1

What country has scored the most World Cup goals?

A. Germany
B. Brazil
C. Argentina

2

Who holds the NFL record for most coaching victories?

A. Don Shula
B. Tom Landry
C. Jimmy Johnson

3

Who holds the NBA record for most career games played?

A. Robert Parish
B. Larry Bird
C. Wilt Chamberlain

SPORTS

4

Which NHL team has the most Stanley Cup victories?

A. New Jersey Devils
B. Detroit Red Wings
C. Montreal Canadiens

5

Which WNBA player has the most career points?

A. Rebecca Lobo
B. Lisa Leslie
C. Sheryl Swoops

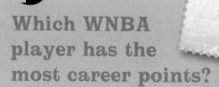

6

Who is the world's top-earning male tennis player?

A. Andre Agassi
B. Bill Tilden
C. Pete Sampras

SPORTS

7

Which professional male golfer has the most tournament wins?

A. Jack Nicklaus
B. Tiger Woods
C. Arnold Palmer

8

Who holds the MLB record for most career games played?

A. Cal Ripkin, Jr.
B. Pete Rose
C. Babe Ruth

9

Who has the fastest Indianapolis 500 win?

A. Rick Mears
B. Al Unser, Jr.
C. Arie Luyendyk

SPORTS

10

Who holds the MLB record for the fastest recorded pitch?

A. Nolan Ryan
B. Randy Johnson
C. Cy Young

11

Who holds the NBA record for the most career points scored?

A. Michael Jordan
B. Shaquille O'Neal
C. Kareem Abdul-Jabbar

12

Who holds the NFL record for leading lifetime scorer?

A. Gary Anderson
B. Jerry Rice
C. Walter Payton

SPORTS

13

What goalie has the most career wins in the NHL?

A. Terry Sawchuck
B. Patrick Roy
C. Ken Dryden

14

What WNBA player has the highest career points per game average?

A. Lisa Leslie
B. Chamique Holdsclaw
C. Cynthia Cooper

15

Who is the world's top-earning female tennis player?

A. Martina Navratilova
B. Steffi Graf
C. Arantxa Sánchez-
Vicario

16

What female soccer player has the most CAPS?

A. Mia Hamm
B. Kristine Lilly
C. Brandi Chastain

17

How many times has Lance Armstrong won the Tour de France?

A. 6
B. 7
C. 9

18

What's the most points an NBA player has scored in one game?

A. 75
B. 125
C. 100

SPORTS

19

Who holds
the MLB
record for
most career
runs?

A. Ty Cobb
B. Ricky Henderson
C. Babe Ruth

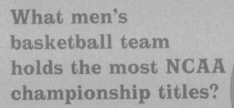

20

Who holds
the record for
being the NFL's
leading lifetime
touchdown
scorer?

A. Jerry Rice
B. Cris Carter
C. Terrell Davis

21

What men's
basketball team
holds the most NCAA
championship titles?

A. UCLA
B. UConn
C. Duke

22

Which NHL team has the largest arena?

A. Tampa Bay Lightning
B. St. Louis Blues
C. New York Rangers

23

How many singles Grand Slam titles does Pete Sampras hold?

A. 9
B. 11
C. 14

24

How many horses run in the Kentucky Derby each year?

A. 10
B. 20
C. 30

SPORTS

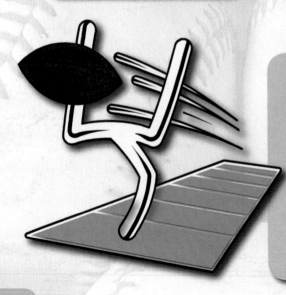

25

Who holds the MLB record for highest career batting average?

A. Babe Ruth
B. Lou Gehrig
C. Ty Cobb

26

Who holds the NBA record for the most career steals?

A. Allen Iverson
B. John Stockton
C. Alvin Robertson

27

What is the longest field goal ever made in the NFL?

A. 63 yards
B. 72 yards
C. 81 yards

28

What NHL player has the most career points?

A. Gordie Howe
B. Wayne Gretzky
C. Mark Messier

29

What country has won the most medals at the Winter Olympics?

A. Sweden
B. Norway
C. Russia

30

Who holds the MLB record for most career strikeouts?

A. Randy Johnson
B. Roger Clemens
C. Nolan Ryan

SPORTS

31

Who holds the NBA record for the most career rebounds?

A. Bill Russell
B. Wilt Chamberlain
C. Kareem Abdul-Jabbar

32

Who is the NFL's leading lifetime passer?

A. Steve Young
B. Kurt Warner
C. Joe Montana

33

What women's basketball team holds the most NCAA championship titles?

A. Tennessee
B. UConn
C. Maryland

SPORTS

34

What is the fastest slap shot recorded in the NHL?

A. 71.7 mph
B. 94.9 mph
C. 118.3 mph

35

Who holds the MLB record for the most career losses?

A. Nolan Ryan
B. Cy Young
C. Walter Johnson

36

Who holds the NBA record for the highest career scoring average?

A. Michael Jordan
B. Jerry West
C. Wilt Chamberlain

SPORTS

37

Who is the NFL's leading lifetime receiver?

A. Cris Carter
B. Jerry Rice
C. Tim Brown

38

What country has won the most medals at the Summer Olympics?

A. China
B. Russia
C. United States

39

What is the most popular sport worldwide?

A. Golf
B. Basketball
C. Soccer

40

Who holds the NBA record for the highest career free throw percentage?

A. Michael Jordan
B. Mark Price
C. Reggie Miller

41

Who holds the NFL record for the most single-season touchdowns?

A. Shaun Alexander
B. Marshall Faulk
C. Priest Holmes

42

What NBA team holds the most championship titles?

A. Detroit Pistons
B. Philadelphia 76ers
C. Boston Celtics

ANIMALS

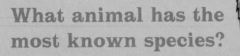

1

What animal has the most known species?

A. Insects
B. Mammals
C. Mollusks

2

What is a group of toads called?

A. Knot
B. Covey
C. Gang

3

What is the only animal that can fly backward?

A. Bat
B. Hummingbird
C. Hawk

4

What is the average distance a caged mouse will run on an exercise wheel each night?

A. 0.5 miles
B. 2.5 miles
C. 10 miles

5

How much can a Komodo dragon eat at one time?

A. Equal to 20% of its body weight
B. Equal to 50% of its body weight
C. Equal to 80% of its body weight

6

How far can a flea jump?

A. 50 times its body length
B. 350 times its body length
C. 700 times its body length

ANIMALS

7

One bite from a black mamba is powerful enough to kill how many humans?

A. 5
B. 50
C. 200

8

How many insects can a bat eat in just one hour?

A. 200
B. 1,200
C. 2,800

9

How long can a saltwater crocodile grow?

A. 10 feet
B. 18 feet
C. 22 feet

10

How many eyes does a grasshopper have?

A. 2
B. 5
C. 8

11

What is an eagle's nest called?

A. Aerie
B. Weave
C. Clash

12

How many lenses make up a dragonfly's eye?

A. 5,000
B. 15,000
C. 30,000

ANIMALS

13

What is the top speed a cheetah can run?

A. 20 mph
B. 65 mph
C. 100 mph

14

What is the most common type of insect?

A. Butterfly
B. Beetle
C. Ant

15

How many olfactory receptors are on a dog's nose?

A. 65 million
B. 220 million
C. 480 million

16

What is the name of a male duck?

A. Drake
B. Gander
C. Cob

18

What do blowflies use to taste foods?

A. Mouth
B. Feet
C. Wings

17

How large in diameter are the eyes of a giant squid?

A.   1 inch
B. 6.5 inches
C. 11 inches

ANIMALS

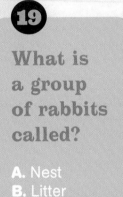

19

What is a group of rabbits called?

A. Nest
B. Litter
C. Pride

20

How many eggs can a queen termite lay in one day?

A. 3,000
B. 18,000
C. 40,000

21

How much water can a camel drink in 10 minutes?

A. 2 gallons
B. 30 gallons
C. 60 gallons

22

How many long feathers does a male peacock have on his back?

A. 80
B. 200
C. 510

23

What U.S. President had an alligator as a pet?

A. Zachary Taylor
B. John Quincy Adams
C. Ulysses S. Grant

24

What is the most popular dog in the United States?

A. Labrador retriever
B. German shepherd
C. Chihuahua

ANIMALS

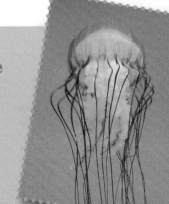

25

How many endangered and threatened species are there in the world?

A. 225
B. 650
C. 1,075

26

How many chicken eggs does it take to equal one ostrich egg?

A. 5
B. 16
C. 24

27

What percentage of a jellyfish is water?

A. 50%
B. 75%
C. 95%

28

How many flowers does a hummingbird visit on an average day?

A. 600
B. 1,000
C. 2,000

30

What animal sleeps the longest each day?

A. Koala
B. Sloth
C. Opossum

29

How many honeybees can live in a beehive at one time?

A. 50,000
B. 70,000
C. 90,000

ANIMALS

32

How far can a kangaroo jump in one leap?

A. 6 feet
B. 20 feet
C. 30 feet

31

What does an ichthyologist study?

A. Fish
B. Mammals
C. Reptiles

33

How far can monarch butterflies migrate each year?

A. 400 miles
B. 1,000 miles
C. 1,800 miles

34

Which animal can move its eyes in two different directions?

A. Chameleons
B. Owls
C. Lobsters

35

How long is a giraffe's tongue?

A. 6 inches
B. 18 inches
C. 26 inches

36

What is the most popular breed of cat in the United States?

A. Persian
B. Siamese
C. Maine Coon

ANIMALS

37

How long can a cockroach live without a head?

A. 1 day
B. 14 days
C. 25 days

38

What is a baby swan called?

A. Cygnet
B. Gosling
C. Chick

39

How many noses does a slug have?

A. 1
B. 2
C. 4

40

How much water can a pelican's pouch hold?

A. 3 gallons
B. 9 gallons
C. 15 gallons

41

How many muscles are in a cat's ear?

A. 12
B. 32
C. 94

42

How long does it take for a chick to develop and hatch from an egg?

A. 21 days
B. 45 days
C. 67 days

ENTERTAINMENT

1

What solo artist holds the record for the most Grammy Awards?

A. Rod Stewart
B. Michael Jackson
C. Stevie Wonder

2

What MTV video has been played more times than any other video in the network's history?

A. *Thriller*
B. *Video Killed the Radio Star*
C. *Sledgehammer*

3

How much has the movie *Titanic* earned worldwide since it opened?

A. $1.05 billion
B. $1.83 billion
C. $2.25 billion

4

How many puppets are used during Disney's *The Lion King* on Broadway?

A. 104
B. 167
C. 232

5

What are the mysterious numbers that frequently appear on *Lost*?

A. 7, 12, 15, 27, 30, 42
B. 4, 8, 15, 16, 23, 42
C. 3, 13, 15, 21, 22, 40

6

What is the longest-running Broadway play?

A. *Cats*
B. *Les Miserables*
C. *The Phantom of the Opera*

7

What percentage of Americans watch television at least once a day?

A. 57%
B. 68%
C. 81%

8

What *Survivor* player did not win $1 million?

A. Ethan Zohn
B. Rob Mariano
C. Jenna Morasca

9

What's the most popular radio format in the United States?

A. Top 40
B. News
C. Country

10

Which movie grossed the most money in the United States during opening weekend?

A. Star Wars: Revenge of the Sith
B. Pirates of the Caribbean: Dead Man's Chest
C. Spider-Man

12

What late-night talk show host brings home the biggest paycheck?

A. Jay Leno
B. Conan O'Brien
C. David Letterman

11

Which band earned the most money in 2005?

A. The Rolling Stones
B. U2
C. Green Day

ENTERTAINMENT

13

Which movie spent the most weeks at the top of the box office charts?

A. *E.T.*
B. *Gone with the Wind*
C. *Titanic*

14

Where do Bart and the rest of the Simpsons live?

A. 417 Evergreen Avenue
B. 174 Springfield Street
C. 714 Evergreen Terrace

15

Which Harry Potter movie has earned the most money worldwide?

A. *Harry Potter and the Sorcerer's Stone*
B. *Harry Potter and the Goblet of Fire*
C. *Harry Potter and the Chamber of Secrets*

16

Which of the seven dwarfs is the only one without a beard?

A. Sneezy
B. Sleepy
C. Dopey

17

What was the first CD created for retail sale in the United States?

A. Born in the USA
B. Thriller
C. 52nd Street

18

What Cameron Diaz movie has earned the most money?

A. Charlie's Angels: Full Throttle
B. Shrek 2
C. There's Something About Mary

ENTERTAINMENT

19

Who won the first Grammy ever given out for a rap performance?

A. Run DMC
B. The Fresh Prince and DJ Jazzy Jeff
C. LL Cool J

21

Who became the first musician to appear on the covers of Time and Newsweek during the same week?

A. Britney Spears
B. Bruce Springsteen
C. Elton John

20

What is the real name of musical pop star Pink?

A. Alex Montana
B. Alecia Moore
C. Ashley Munson

22

Who was the first artist to have a number one movie and a number one album on the same weekend?

A. Jennifer Lopez
B. Britney Spears
C. Madonna

23

How many sketches were drawn for the hit movie *Cars*?

A. 17,000
B. 43,000
C. 71,000

24

Who is the youngest winner of a Grammy Award?

A. Madonna
B. LeAnn Rimes
C. Mariah Carey

ENTERTAINMENT

25

Who provides the voice for Marty the Zebra in *Madagascar?*

A. Ben Stiller
B. Chris Rock
C. Bruce Willis

26

What female artist has the most gold album awards in the United States?

A. Madonna
B. Barbra Streisand
C. Celine Dion

27

What Jim Carrey movie has earned the most money?

A. *How the Grinch Stole Christmas*
B. *Bruce Almighty*
C. *Liar Liar*

ENTERTAINMENT

28

What is the fictional town that Rory and Lorelai call home on *Gilmore Girls*?

A. Stars Hollow
B. Sleepy Hollow
C. Sunny Hollow

29

Who was the first musical act ever to play at Yankee Stadium?

A. Sheryl Crow
B. U2
C. Billy Joel

30

What movie star has the most movies that have grossed at least $100 million?

A. Tom Cruise
B. Bruce Willis
C. Julia Roberts

32

Who was the first singer to have her first five singles hit number one on the *Billboard* Hot 100 chart?

A. Britney Spears
B. Whitney Houston
C. Mariah Carey

31

How much does it cost to buy a vowel on *Wheel of Fortune*?

A. $150
B. $200
C. $250

33

Who's America's top-paid model?

A. Tyra Banks
B. Kate Moss
C. Gisele Bundchen

Which movie had the biggest pre-approved budget?

A. *Superman Returns*
B. *Titanic*
C. *Waterworld*

35

Where does SpongeBob SquarePants live?

A. Bikini Bottom
B. Beluga Bay
C. Barnacle Beach

36

Who is the first character to speak in *Star Wars*?

A. Han Solo
B. R2D2
C. C-3PO

37

What is Donald Duck's middle name?

A. Francis
B. Fauntleroy
C. Ferdinand

38

How much did a 30-second commercial cost during Super Bowl XL in 2006?

A. $1.9 million
B. $2.5 million
C. $3.4 million

39

How many albums has Celine Dion sold worldwide?

A. 80 million
B. 115 million
C. 175 million

40

Which deceased celebrity still earns more than $40 million each year?

A. Elvis Presley
B. John Lennon
C. Marilyn Monroe

41

Which movie earned the most money in 2005?

A. *Star Wars: Episode III - Revenge of the Sith*
B. *Harry Potter and the Goblet of Fire*
C. *The Chronicles of Narnia: The Lion, the Witch and the Wardrobe*

42

Which is not an MTV Movie Awards category?

A. Best Frightened Performance
B. Best On Screen Team
C. Best Animal Performance

HUMAN BODY

1

If all the nerves in an adult's body were strung together, how long would they measure?

A. 4 miles
B. 47 miles
C. 147 miles

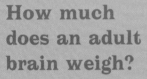

2

How much does an adult brain weigh?

A. 3 pounds
B. 10 pounds
C. 18 pounds

3

How many hairs are on an adult's body?

A. 100,000
B. 5 million
C. 25 million

4

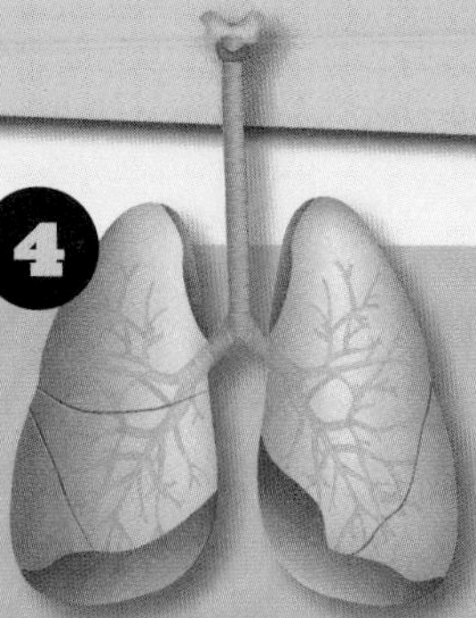

How many miles of airways bring air in and out of the lungs?

A. 1,500
B. 2,500
C. 3,500

5

What is the most active muscle group in the body?

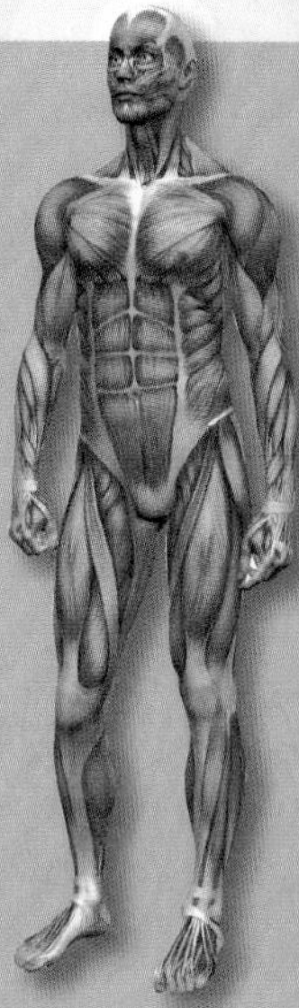

A. Heart
B. Leg
C. Eye

6

How many breaths does a kid take in a minute?

A. 2
B. 10
C. 20

HUMAN BODY

7

What is the longest bone in the human body?

A. Tibia
B. Femur
C. Humerus

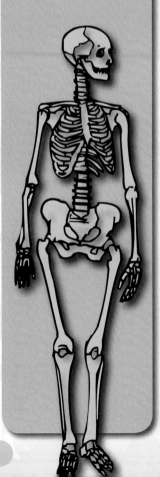

8

How many different smells can a human nose distinguish between?

A. 800
B. 5,000
C. 10,000

9

How much skin does a person shed in a lifetime?

A. 10 pounds
B. 40 pounds
C. 75 pounds

10

How many gallons of blood flow through the kidneys each day?

A. 76 gallons
B. 210 gallons
C. 440 gallons

11

What percentage of the brain is water?

A. 10%
B. 45%
C. 85%

12

What is the only bone not connected to another in the body?

A. Hyoid bone
B. Pisiform bone
C. Hamate bone

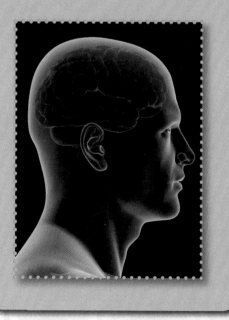

HUMAN BODY

13

How many muscles does it take to frown?

A. 4
B. 21
C. 47

14

How much blood does the average man have?

A. 5 to 6 liters
B. 10 to 11 liters
C. 19 to 20 liters

15

How many bones are in the human hand?

A. 8
B. 27
C. 44

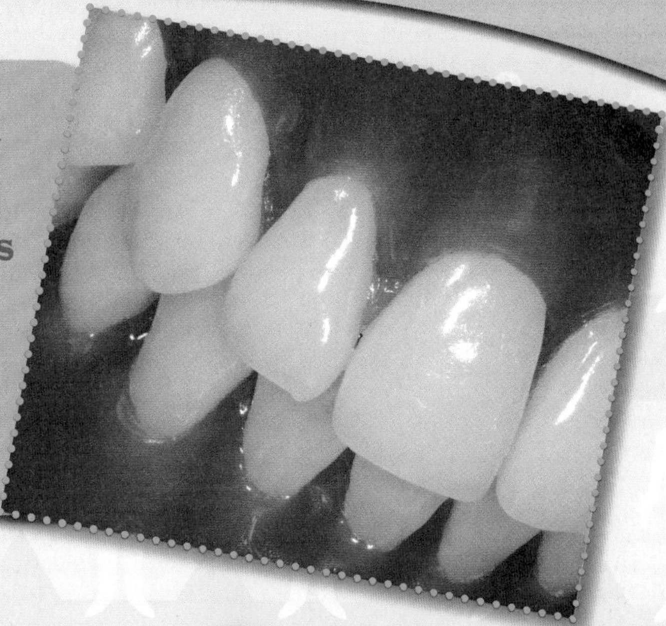

16

How many teeth do most adults have?

A. 18
B. 32
C. 40

17

On average, how many dreams do adults have each night?

A. 5
B. 10
C. 15

18

What is the largest solid organ in the body?

A. Stomach
B. Liver
C. Heart

ANATOMY

HUMAN BODY

19

How much saliva can a person produce in a lifetime?

A. 2,000 gallons
B. 10,000 gallons
C. 18,000 gallons

20

How often does an adult's blood circulate through his or her body each day?

A. 225 times
B. 1,500 times
C. 2,750 times

21

What percentage of your body weight is blood?

A. 10%
B. 25%
C. 40%

22

How many times does your heart beat during one day?

A. 50,000
B. 100,000
C. 150,000

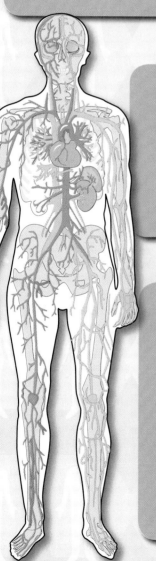

23

What is the largest artery in the body?

A. Aorta
B. Capillary
C. Jugular

24

If an adult's blood vessels were strung together, how many times would they circle the Earth?

A. 0.5
B. 2.5
C. 4.0

25

How many hairs fall out of a person's head on an average day?

A. 10
B. 80
C. 175

26

How many cells make up an average adult's body?

A. 1 million
B. 1 billion
C. 1 trillion

27

How many bones are in an adult's body?

A. 75
B. 206
C. 412

28

How much skin does an adult have?

A. 20 square feet
B. 50 square feet
C. 75 square feet

29

What is the hardest substance in the body?

A. Bone
B. Cartilage
C. Enamel

30

How much food can an adult's stomach hold?

A. 1.5 liters
B. 5.5 liters
C. 9.0 liters

31

How many functions does the liver perform?

A. 50
B. 200
C. 500

32

What is the smallest bone in your body?

A. Stirrup
B. Toe bone
C. Hammer

33

What is the average speed of a cough?

A. 5 miles per hour
B. 35 miles per hour
C. 60 miles per hour

34

When is your sense of smell the weakest?

A. Morning
B. Noon
C. Night

35

How long is an adult's small intestine?

A. 2 feet
B. 12 feet
C. 22 feet

36

How long does a fingernail take to grow from base to tip?

A. 1 month
B. 6 months
C. 12 months

37

What is the fastest-growing hair on the body?

A. Eyelashes
B. Beard
C. Leg

38

How many bacteria are found on one square inch of the body?

A. 5 million
B. 32 million
C. 57 million

39

How much blood does a human heart pump in an hour?

A. 300 quarts
B. 900 quarts
C. 1,500 quarts

40

What is the only organ that can float on water?

A. Lungs
B. Bladder
C. Kidney

41

How many taste buds are in an adult's mouth?

A. 1,000
B. 10,000
C. 20,000

42

How many times a day does the average person blink?

A. 3,520
B. 10,940
C. 17,280

STATISTICS

1

What are the odds of giving birth to twins?

A. 1 in 33
B. 1 in 303
C. 1 in 3,300

2

What percentage of the kids in the United States are homeschooled?

A. 2%
B. 24%
C. 42%

3

What are your odds of being killed by a bolt of lightning?

A. 1 in 900
B. 1 in 71,500
C. 1 in 800,000

4

What percentage of dog owners buy Christmas presents for their pets?

A. 25%
B. 50%
C. 70%

6

What are the odds of catching a foul ball in the stands at a baseball game?

A. 1 in 17
B. 1 in 563
C. 1 in 5,083

5

What are the odds of being hit by an asteroid from space?

A. 1 in 50,000
B. 1 in 100,000
C. 1 in 200,000

STATISTICS

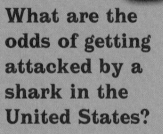

7

What are the odds of becoming President of the United States?

A. 1 in 850,000
B. 1 in 4 million
C. 1 in 10 million

8

What are the odds of getting attacked by a shark in the United States?

A. 1 in 2,700
B. 1 in 943,000
C. 1 in 6 million

9

What percentage of applicants get accepted to Harvard?

A. 1%
B. 12%
C. 26%

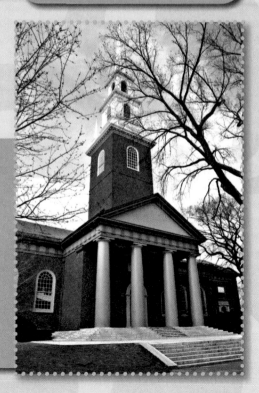

10

What percentage of public elementary schools sells soda?

A. 12%
B. 34%
C. 68%

11

What percentage of kids age 4 through 12 has a television in their bedroom?

A. 4%
B. 48%
C. 79%

12

What are the odds of finding a four-leaf clover?

A. 1 in 4,000
B. 1 in 10,000
C. 1 in 18,000

13

What percentage of Americans chooses chocolate as their favorite ice cream flavor?

A. 12%
B. 32%
C. 52%

14

What percentage of children in the United States dresses up for Halloween?

A. 31%
B. 55%
C. 82%

15

What percentage of worldwide Internet usage does the United States account for?

A. 18%
B. 31%
C. 64%

16

What are the odds of a book reaching the *New York Times* best-sellers list?

A. 1 in 8
B. 1 in 220
C. 1 in 865

17

What percentage of the world's amateur photographs is taken at Walt Disney World?

A. 4%
B. 22%
C. 40%

18

What percentage of cars in the United States are silver?

A. 8%
B. 26%
C. 41%

19

What percentage of sales revenue does rock music account for in cassette and CD sales?

A. 4%
B. 15%
C. 24%

20

What percentage of American homes have three or more television sets?

A. 12%
B. 23%
C. 46%

21

What percentage of kids age 6 to 17 participates in extracurricular activities in the United States?

A. 27%
B. 59%
C. 88%

22

What percentage of Miss America winners is from California?

A. 7%
B. 18%
C. 30%

23

What percentage of worldwide space launches has been commanded by the United States?

A. 29%
B. 57%
C. 84%

24

What percentage of American families watches television while eating dinner?

A. 21%
B. 63%
C. 89%

STATISTICS

25

What are the odds of a person working in the movie industry winning an Academy Award?

A. 1 in 2,000
B. 1 in 6,800
C. 1 in 11,500

26

What percentage of the toy market do video games account for?

A. 28%
B. 49%
C. 61%

27

What percentage of Americans pay to watch at least one movie in their homes each week?

A. 8%
B. 40%
C. 71%

28

What percentage of babies are girls?

A. 47.2%
B. 48.8%
C. 50.1%

29

What percentage of Americans thinks the penny should be taken out of circulation?

A. 3%
B. 23%
C. 59%

30

What percentage of Americans claims to exercise on a weekly basis?

A. 20%
B. 43%
C. 67%

STATISTICS

31

What percentage of the day does the average American spend in front of the television?

A. 3%
B. 32%
C. 67%

32

What percentage of climbers reaches the top of Mount Everest?

A. 20%
B. 50%
C. 80%

33

What percentage of holiday gift-givers waits until the day before Christmas to do their shopping?

A. 7%
B. 23%
C. 47%

VOLUNTEERS WELCOME
PLEASE CHECK AT OFFICE

34

What percentage of adults in the United States participates in charity work?

A. 14%
B. 35%
C. 51%

35

What are the odds of a PGA golfer sinking a hole in one?

A. 1 in 37
B. 1 in 9,048
C. 1 in 2,491

36

What percentage of American households owns a bird?

A. 5%
B. 20%
C. 36%

37

What percentage of the sneaker market do kids age 14 and under account for?

A. 10%
B. 30%
C. 50%

39

What percentage of advertising is done in the newspaper?

A. 18%
B. 39%
C. 54%

38

What percentage of adults reads books two or more times a week?

A. 3%
B. 20%
C. 45%

40

What percentage of U.S. families barbecues each summer?

A. 8%
B. 15%
C. 32%

41

What are the odds of becoming a professional athlete?

A. 1 in 1,000
B. 1 in 22,000
C. 1 in 96,000

42

What percentage of American homes has a DVD player?

A. 18%
B. 44%
C. 76%

SCIENCE

1

How long does it take for light from the Sun to reach Earth?

A. 8.3 minutes
B. 35.6 minutes
C. 94.1 minutes

2

What does NASA stand for?

NASA

A. National Aeronautics and Space Administration
B. Notable Assembly of Scientific Administration
C. National Association of Space Astronauts

3

What color star is the hottest?

A. Blue
B. Red
C. Yellow

SCIENCE

4

How many constellations are in the sky?

A. 88
B. 390
C. 617

5

At what temperature will water freeze?

A. 12 °F
B. 32 °F
C. 48 °F

6

How much do Earth's plates move each year?

A. 2.2 inches
B. 39.4 inches
C. 108.1 inches

SCIENCE

7

What is the deepest part of the world's oceans?

A. The Middle America Trench in the Pacific Ocean
B. The Puerto Rico Trench in the Atlantic Ocean
C. The Mariana Trench in the Pacific Ocean

8

How many feet can the Bay of Fundy in Canada rise at high tide?

A. 8 feet
B. 55 feet
C. 199 feet

9

What is the most common element in the Earth's crust?

A. Silica
B. Oxygen
C. Aluminum

How many stars are in our galaxy?

A. 20 billion
B. 60 billion
C. 100 billion

What is the hottest temperature ever recorded on Earth?

A. 96 °F
B. 136 °F
C. 161 °F

How hot is a bolt of lightning?

A. 13,000 °F
B. 54,000 °F
C. 97,000 °F

SCINCE

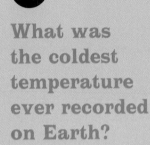

13

What was the coldest temperature ever recorded on Earth?

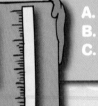

A. -57.9 °F
B. -94.2 °F
C. -128.6 °F

14

What is the longest land mountain range?

A. The Andes Mountains
B. The White Mountains
C. The Appalachian Mountains

15

What item is not allowed on the Space Shuttle?

A. Movie
B. Chocolate
C. Teddy Bear

16

How many earthquakes occur around the world each year?

A. 125,000
B. 500,000
C. 750,000

17

What items make up the largest percentage of Americans' trash?

A. Plastic packaging and wraps
B. Paper products and cardboard
C. Diapers

18

How long does it take for the Space Shuttle to reach a speed of 17,000 miles per hour?

A. 8 minutes
B. 29 minutes
C. 47 minutes

United States

SCIENCE

19

What country has the greatest oil reserves?

A. Iraq
B. Canada
C. Saudi Arabia

20

On average, how many inches of precipitation fall in a tropical rain forest annually?

A. 38 inches
B. 70 inches
C. 136 inches

21

What two compounds combine to make water?

A. Helium and Nitrogen
B. Hydrogen and Oxygen
C. Nitrogen and Oxygen

22

What does an agronomist study?

A. Trees and bushes
B. Precipitation and runoff
C. Soil and agriculture

23

The asteroid belt is located between which two planets?

A. Mercury and Venus
B. Mars and Jupiter
C. Earth and Neptune

24

A tornado's winds can reach up to what speed?

A. 130 miles per hour
B. 300 miles per hour
C. 420 miles per hour

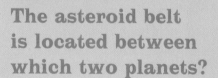

SCIENCE

25

What is the highest recorded snowfall for a single location in one season?

A. 329 inches
B. 710 inches
C. 1,140 inches

26

How many different types of flowering plants are in the world?

A. 95,000
B. 149,000
C. 250,000

27

In what year did American astronauts first land on the moon?

A. 1949
B. 1969
C. 1979

SCIENCE

28

What is the oldest living type of tree in the United States?

A. Bristlecone Pine
B. Douglas Fir
C. Giant Sequoia

29

How fast does the Earth move around the Sun?

A. 8,400 miles per hour
B. 31,650 miles per hour
C. 67,000 miles per hour

30

What is the diameter of the world's largest flower, the Rafflesia?

A. 0.5 feet
B. 3 feet
C. 8 feet

SCIENCE

**How much
of the world's
water is located
in the oceans?**

A. 51%
B. 78%
C. 97%

**What percentage
of the Earth is
covered by
rain forest?**

A. 7%
B. 20%
C. 36%

**How many
millions of
cubic miles
of ice are on
Earth?**

A. 1 million
B. 9 million
C. 22 million

34

How many active volcanoes are located around the world?

A. 1,500
B. 6,500
C. 10,500

36

What was the first animal to visit space?

A. Rabbit
B. Dog
C. Chimp

35

During which era did dinosaurs roam the Earth?

A. Paleozoic
B. Mesozoic
C. Cenozoic

SCIENCE

37

What tool is not included in an astronaut's space suit?

A. Life raft
B. Parachute
C. Chewing gum

38

What gas makes up 78% of the atmosphere?

A. Nitrogen
B. Hydrogen
C. Oxygen

39

How many acres of rain forest are destroyed each minute?

A. 30 acres
B. 75 acres
C. 145 acres

What are Saturn's rings made out of?

A. Meteors and ash
B. Ice, dust, and rock
C. Smoke and charred particles

Which state has the most earthquakes?

A. California
B. Washington
C. Alaska

How many trees does it take to create all of the newspapers in the United States annually?

A. 10 million
B. 30 million
C. 50 million

WORLD

1

Which country is the largest by area?

A. China
B. Russia
C. Canada

2

Which country is the smallest by area?

A. Vatican City
B. Monaco
C. Liechtenstein

3

Where is Mount Everest—the world's highest elevation—located?

A. Nepal
B. Switzerland
C. Tibet

4

What country has the most coastline?

A. Canada
B. China
C. Australia

5

Which ocean is the largest?

A. Atlantic
B. Indian
C. Pacific

6

What country has the highest life expectancy?

A. Japan
B. Singapore
C. Andorra

WORLD

7

What is the largest island in the world?

A. Madagascar
B. Great Britain
C. Greenland

9

What is the longest river in the world?

A. Amazon
B. Nile
C. Huang He

8

Where is Angel Falls—the world's highest waterfall—located?

A. Norway
B. Venezuela
C. New Zealand

10

What country has the highest population of young people?

A. Chad
B. Uganda
C. Democratic Republic
   of Congo

11

Which is the world's most populous country?

A. India
B. Bangladesh
C. China

12

What is the world's most populous city?

A. Seoul, Korea
B. Moscow, Russia
C. Tokyo, Japan

WORLD

Which is the world's largest continent?

A. Asia
B. Africa
C. Europe

What country has the lowest population?

A. Tuvalu
B. Nauru
C. Palau

15

Where is the Sahara— the world's largest desert— located?

A. Australia
B. Africa
C. South America

16

What country attracts the most tourists each year?

A. France
B. Spain
C. United States

17

What is the most commonly spoken language in the world?

A. Mandarin Chinese
B. Spanish
C. English

18

What country has the highest population of people over the age of 65?

A. Japan
B. Monaco
C. Italy

WORLD

19

What country has the longest border?

A. China
B. United States
C. Russia

20

What country has the most forest area?

A. Canada
B. Russia
C. Brazil

21

How many of the states in the United States end in the letter A?

A. 12
B. 21
C. 34

22

What country has the most marriages each year?

A. United States
B. Japan
C. Russia

24

What country eats the most chocolate?

A. Belgium
B. Switzerland
C. Germany

23

What two countries are tied for bordering the most neighboring countries?

A. China & Brazil
B. Russia & China
C. Germany & Brazil

WORLD

25

How many countries are in the world?

A. 107
B. 193
C. 282

27

How many countries have English as an official language?

A. 8
B. 29
C. 57

26

Which country is entirely a desert?

A. Djibouti
B. Botswana
C. Saudi Arabia

28

What is the total land area on the Earth?

A. 11.6 million square miles
B. 23.7 million square miles
C. 57.5 million square miles

30

What country has the most Internet users?

A. China
B. United States
C. Japan

29

What country publishes the world's most-read newspaper?

A. China
B. Brazil
C. Japan

WORLD

31

Where is the world's tallest volcano?

A. Chile
B. Alaska
C. Argentina

33

In what country is the world's largest library located?

A. China
B. United States
C. Russia

32

What country has the most cell phone users worldwide?

A. Iceland
B. Finland
C. Luxembourg

34

What is the largest lake in the world?

A. Lake Victoria
B. Lake Superior
C. Caspian Sea

35

What is the longest cave system in the world?

A. Mammoth Cave
B. Carlsbad Cave
C. Waitomo Cave

36

Which country has the highest average level of schooling?

A. Norway
B. Finland
C. Australia

37

The citizens of which country donate the most to charitable causes?

A. Denmark
B. United States
C. Luxembourg

38

How much of Antarctica is covered by ice?

A. 57%
B. 71%
C. 98%

39

What country mails the most letters?

A. China
B. Vatican City
C. United States

40

What is the lowest elevation on Earth?

A. Death Valley, United States
B. Dead Sea, Jordan
C. Lake Assal, Djibouti

41

What country watches the most television?

A. United States
B. Thailand
C. Italy

42

How large is the continent of North America?

A. 9.4 million square miles
B. 38.1 million square miles
C. 55.8 million square miles

TOYS

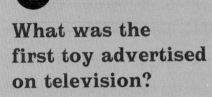

1

What was the first toy advertised on television?

A. Barbie
B. Mr. Potato Head
C. Slinky

2

How much sheet metal does Tonka use each year to make its trucks?

A. 100,000 pounds
B. 1.7 million pounds
C. 5.1 million pounds

3

How many Barbie dolls are sold per second worldwide?

A. 3 dolls every second
B. 40 dolls every second
C. 100 dolls every second

4

How many Silly Putty eggs are made each day?

A. 20,000
B. 210,000
C. 1,000,000

5

How many words can be used to score points in a Scrabble game?

A. 3,800
B. 147,000
C. 549,200

6

What is the best-selling Hot Wheels vehicle?

A. Police car
B. Camaro
C. Corvette

7

How many crayons will a child wear down by his or her tenth birthday?

A. 44
B. 730
C. 3,409

8

What was Play-Doh originally used for?

A. Tile grout
B. Wallpaper cleaner
C. Plumber's sealer

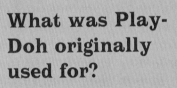

9

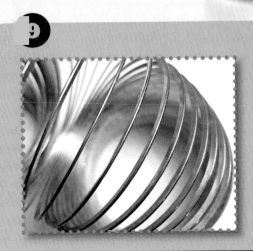

How long does it take to produce a Slinky?

A. 10 seconds
B. 18 minutes
C. 75 minutes

10

How long has the yo-yo been around?

A. 82 years
B. 900 years
C. 3,000 years

11

What was depicted on the first jigsaw puzzle?

A. World map
B. Basket of kittens
C. Christmas scene

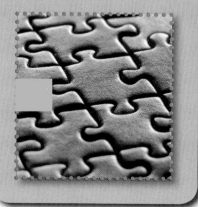

12

What were the first dolls that could shut their eyes?

A. Madame Alexander dolls
B. Chatty Cathy dolls
C. Kewpie dolls

13

How much do Americans spend on toys annually?

A. $4 billion
B. $21 billion
C. $37 billion

14

If all the Playmobil vehicles ever produced were lined up end to end, how far would they stretch?

A. From New York to California
B. 1.5 times around Earth
C. The distance between Mars and Jupiter

15

How many Trivial Pursuit games have been sold worldwide?

A. 30 million
B. 75 million
C. 100 million

16

Jenga—a balancing game using wood pieces—is a word from what language?

A. Swahili
B. Latin
C. Ethiopian

17

What toy was developed by the son of famous architect Frank Lloyd Wright?

A. Lincoln Logs
B. Tinker Toys
C. K'Nex

18

When was the first board game produced in the United States?

A. 1804
B. 1843
C. 1917

TOYS

19

Where did the game Parcheesi originate?

A. China
B. India
C. Pakistan

20

How much do Americans spend on video games each year?

A. $1.8 billion
B. $6.2 billion
C. $10.5 billion

21

What special toy did the astronauts on Apollo 8 take with them?

A. Rubik's Cube
B. Etch-A-Sketch
C. Silly Putty

23

What everyday object inspired the Frisbee?

A. Hubcap
B. Garbage can lid
C. Pie plate

22

What is Barbie's middle name?

A. Marie
B. Millicent
C. Madison

MALIBU™ 110G. MODEL

FRISBEE®DISC

24

What is the name of the hero in The Legend of Zelda?

A. Link
B. Zeus
C. Coal

TOYS

25

How many color combinations are possible for a Rubik's Cube?

A.   1,483,654,184
B.   30,294,602,145,122
C. 43,252,003,274,489,856,000

26

What is inside an Etch-A-Sketch?

A. Plastic beads and aluminum powder
B. Lead bits and ground tin
C. Carbon and graphite

27

What is the total amount of money included in a Monopoly game?

A. $15,140
B. $40,500
C. $90,170

28

How many Hot Wheels cars have been produced since they debuted in 1968?

A. 870 million
B. 1.5 billion
C. 8.7 billion

30

How many boys in the United States own a G.I. Joe action figure?

A. 1 out of 15
B. 1 out of 7
C. 2 out of 3

29

How many different ways are there to combine six 8-stud LEGO bricks?

A. 800,291
B. 102,981,500
C. 941,300,450

31

What was Twister's original name?

A. Pretzel
B. Stretch
C. Tangle

32

How many Candy Land games have been sold since it debuted in 1949?

A. 12 million
B. 40 million
C. 145 million

33

Which of the following is *not* a weapon in the game Clue?

A. Lead pipe
B. Wrench
C. Brick

34

How many possible missions are in RISK?

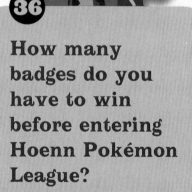

A. 7
B. 28
C. 53

35

Which of the following is *not* a response from the Magic 8 Ball?

A. Ask Again Later
B. Signs Point to Yes
C. I Have No Idea

36

How many badges do you have to win before entering Hoenn Pokémon League?

A. 3
B. 8
C. 16

TOYS

37

In The Game of Life, which of the possible careers only appears on one tile?

A. Police Officer
B. Doctor
C. President

38

What is the bestselling video game of all time?

A. Super Mario Bros.
B. The Legend of Zelda
C. Donkey Kong

39

What toy was used during World War II for military training?

A. G.I. Joe
B. View Masters
C. Battleship

40

Which of the following was not one of the original nine Beanie Babies?

A. Cubbie the Bear
B. Spot the Dog
C. Squeaker the Mouse

41

What game was often included in the tomb when a pharaoh died in ancient Egypt?

A. Chess
B. Backgammon
C. Checkers

42

What is the highest possible word score in Scrabble?

A. 70 points
B. 119 points
C. 164 points

ANSWERS

1. It takes 12 honeybees to collect enough nectar to make just one teaspoon of honey. A bee visits between 100 to 1,500 flowers before returning to the hive and transferring the nectar to worker bees.

2. Some 350 slices of pizzas are eaten in the United States every second. That's equivalent to 100 acres of pizza each day. Every person in the country eats about 46 slices each year, resulting in approximately 3 billion pizzas sold annually.

3. There are approximately 800 kernels arranged in 16 rows on a corn cob. It takes about 1,300 kernels to make up one pound. One bushel of corn can be used to sweeten more than 400 cans of soda.

4. One cow can produce about 35,000 glasses of milk each year. That's the equivalent of 18,806 pounds or about 2,187 gallons. In one cow's lifetime, it will produce about 700,000 glasses of milk— or enough to give a glass to each person living in Austin, Texas.

5. Squid is the most popular pizza topping in Japan. Some of the country's other favorite pizza toppings include eel, mashed potatoes, mayonnaise, hard-boiled eggs, and corn.

6. Approximately 87 billion eggs are produced in the United States each year. That's enough to give every person in the country 300 eggs each! There are about 276 million laying hens in the United States, which means each hen lays about 315 eggs each year.

7. An adult will eat 1,500 pounds of food each year. That adds up to about 90,000 pounds during the average American's lifespan. That's about the same total as 20 full-grown hippopotamuses.

8. There are approximately 100,000 bacteria in one glass of drinking water. However, the vast majority of the bacteria is harmless to ingest and does not pose a threat to people.

9. Americans buy more candy for Halloween than any other holiday. Approximately 10% of the candy market's sales occur at this time of the year, often totaling about $7 billion. Top sellers are the miniature Snickers, Reese's Peanut Butter Cups, and Kit Kats.

10. Los Angeles, California, has the highest hot dog sales with about 41.6 million units sold each year. Weiner sales in the city total more than $81.9 million.

11. More Americans—almost two-thirds of all chocolate eaters—like milk chocolate best. Approximately 90% of adults in the

United States enjoy chocolate. About 59% of kids ages 9-12 and 46% of kids ages 6-8 enjoy eating chocolate as well.

12. California produces approximately 186 billion gallons of ice cream each year. The state has everything needed for a successful ice cream business—about 2,000 dairies, some 1.5 million cows, and 35 ice cream plants.

13. Approximately 8 billion conversation hearts are produced for Valentine's Day each year. Although the candy is only sold for about 6 weeks during the year, it is produced for the 11 months leading up to the February holiday.

14. There are about 7,000 pieces of fruit on an average cherry tree. The two main types of cherry trees are wild cherries that produce sweet fruit, and sour cherries that produce fruit that is usually used for jams or cooking.

15. About 1.3 million pounds of dry pasta are sold in the United States annually. This results in about $235 million each year. The average American eats pasta about 40 times a year.

16. It takes about 850 peanuts to make a jar of peanut butter. About half of the United States' peanut crop is turned into peanut butter. Americans eat enough of the sticky sandwich spread to make more than 10 billion PB&Js annually.

17. There are 40,000 different varieties of rice grown around the world. Rice is the world's third-largest food crop and is the main diet of half the world's population. It is also used for animal bedding, fuels, and paper.

18. Per capita, Americans drink more than 52 gallons of soda each year. That averages about 557 cans of pop annually, which accounts for about one-quarter of all beverages consumed in the country.

19. China produces about 70 million tons of fruit annually, which is about 15% of the world's total production. China is the top producer of apples and pears, and earns about $13 billion annually.

20. There are approximately 555,750 fast-food restaurants in China. The most popular restaurants in the country are KFC, McDonald's, California Fried Chicken, and Pizza Hut.

21. McDonald's operates more than 30,500 franchises worldwide. Located in 119 different countries, McDonald's serves about 50 million customers each day.

22. There are approximately 200 seeds on a strawberry. These tiny seeds are very unusual, however, because they grow on the outside of the fruit.

ANSWERS

23. Americans eat more than 33 pounds of bananas each year. That's about 1 banana every three days. Stacked end to end, this many bananas would stand taller than an 8-story building.

24. It takes 5.25 gallons of milk to make one pound of cheese. A cow will produce enough milk each month to make 210 pounds of cheese. In the United States, people eat an average of 31 pounds of cheese annually.

25. The original name of Pepsi Cola was Brad's Drink, after the drink's founder, Caleb Bradhem. The formula was renamed Pepsi Cola in 1898.

26. More burgers are sold in restaurants on Saturday than any other day of the week. Some 1.4 billion burgers are eaten on that day annually. And, about 75% of those burgers are served with cheese.

27. Vanilla is the most popular ice cream flavor, accounting for about 25% of the market. Chocolate is the second most popular with about 10% of the market. The most-used ice cream topping is chocolate syrup.

28. A lollipop machine can produce 5,900 of the tasty treats per minute. That's about 8.5 million pops in just one day—enough to give everyone living in all of New York City a yummy snack.

29. Every year, 7-Eleven serves close to 100 million fresh grilled hot dogs to its customers. To wash down all those dogs, the convenience store sells 139 million Slurpees, 33 million gallons of soft drinks, and 365 million cups of coffee.

30. Krispy Kreme turns out 7.5 million doughnuts each day. That's about 2.7 billion delicious breakfast snacks ann-ually—enough to treat everyone in the United States to nine doughnuts.

31. A person will eat approxi-mately 160 bowls of cereal a year. Some 49% of the population starts the morning off with cereal. Some 2.7 billion boxes are sold each year, making cereal the third-most-purchased item in grocery stores.

32. It takes 28,800 Oreos to span the length of the Golden Gate

Bridge. The cookie, which measures 1.75 inches long, is the most popular brand in the country. More than 20.5 million are consumed each day.

33. It takes 2.7 million cans of soda to fill up an Olympic-sized pool. At 12 ounces a can, it would take 112,500 cases of pop to equal the 253,125-gallon pool.

34. It would take 60,235 boxes of Barnum's Animal Crackers to equal the weight of an African elephant. The box, which weighs 2.125 ounces, has 22 cookies inside and has featured 55 different animals since 1902.

35. A can of soda contains 9 teaspoons of sugar. That's almost three-fourths of a teaspoon per ounce of soda. The USDA recommends that people do not eat more than 10 teaspoons of sugar in one day.

36. Baseball fans will eat about 27.5 million hot dogs at parks during the season. That's enough to stretch from Los Angeles to Philadelphia. Some 32% of hot dog eaters prefer mustard on top, followed by 23% who pick ketchup.

37. Each year, more than 36 million heart-shaped boxes of candy are sold for Valentine's Day. About 49% of Americans celebrating the holiday buy candy for someone, totaling more than $1 billion in sales.

38. Hamburgers are the most popular grilled items, followed by steak and chicken. In fact, one in every five times someone fires up the grill, it's to cook a burger. About 73% of all burgers eaten in America are prepared at home.

39. It takes about 50 licks for a kid to finish a scoop of ice cream. Kids under 13 eat about half of all prepackaged ice cream novelties.

40. As of March 2003, the state of Illinois adopted popcorn as its official snack food. But it's not only Illinois residents who enjoy it—Americans consume more than 17.3 billion quarts annually.

41. An airline serves about 93 million bags of peanuts each year. An airline also serves about 4 million bags of pretzels, 55 million cans of soda, and 14 million snack packs.

42. Park-goers eat more than 9 million pounds of French fries annually. Disney also uses 1.2 million pounds of watermelon, some 510,000 pounds of grapes, about 1.2 million pounds of sugar, and another 2.9 million pounds of eggs each year.

ANSWERS

PAGES 18–31

1. Brazil has accumulated 30 goals in World Cup competition. Brazil's World Cup wins came between 1958 and 2002.

2. Don Shula won 347 games during his 33-year career. He ended his coaching career with a overall percentage of .677. Shula coached the Miami Dolphins and the Indianapolis Colts.

3. Robert Parish played 1,611 games during his career. At 43, he is the oldest person to have played in the NBA. During his 21 seasons, he played for the Golden State Warriors, Boston Celtics, Charlotte Hornets, and Chicago Bulls.

4. Between 1916 and 1993, the Montreal Canadians have won the Stanley Cup 24 times. That's about 25% of all of the championships ever played!

5. Lisa Leslie has scored 4,732 points in her WNBA career. Leslie is a center for the Los Angeles Sparks and averages 17.3 points per game. She also picked up two gold medals at the Olympic Games in 1996 and 2000.

6. Pete Sampras has earned more than $43 million since he turned professional in 1990. That equals $377.60 an hour for 13 years.

7. Jack Nicklaus has won 18 major tournaments between 1963 and 1986. His wins include 6 Masters, 5 PGAs, 4 U.S. Opens, and 3 British Opens.

8. Pete Rose played in 3,562 games during his career. He is also the all-time leader in hits (4,256) and at bats (14,053). Rose appeared in 17 All Star Games, and was in 3 World Series.

9. Arie Luyendyk averaged a speed of 185.98 miles per hour when he won the Indy 500 in 1990. This was Luyendyk's first Indy race, and he later went on to win another in 1997.

10. Nolan Ryan threw a 100.9-mile-an-hour pitch in 1974. Ryan was a California Angel playing against the Chicago White Sox.

11. During his career, Kareem Abdul Jabbar scored 38,387 points. The 7-foot center's career spanned from 1965 to 1989, during which he played for UCLA, the Milwaukee Bucks, and the LA Lakers.

12. Gary Anderson scored 2,434 points during his 23-year career. Anderson was a kicker and played for the Pittsburgh Steelers, the Philadelphia Eagles, the San Francisco 49ers, the Minnesota Vikings, and the Tennessee Titans.

13. Patrick Roy has won 551 games as a goalie in the NHL. Roy also holds the record for career games played (1,029), career playoff wins (151), and career play-off games played (247).

14. Cynthia Cooper averaged 21.0 points per game as a guard for the Houston Comets. Cooper played in the league from 1997 to 2000, and then came back in 2003 for four games before going back into retirement.

15. Steffi Graf has earned $21.8 million during her 17-year professional career. She's won 22 Grand Slam singles titles and 107 tournament titles.

16. Kristine Lilly has 300 CAPS, or international games played. Lilly has played more than 23,000 hours for the U.S. National Team since she began playing in 1987.

17. Lance Armstrong has won the Tour de France seven times. His wins came between 1999 and 2005. Armstrong retired in 2005.

18. On March 2, 1962, Philadelphia Warriors center Wilt Chamberlain scored 100 points against the New York Knicks in Hershey, Pennsylvania.

19. Ricky Henderson had 2,295 runs during his career. He also leads the league in stolen bases (1,406) and game-opening home runs (81).

20. Jerry Rice has a total of 208 career touchdowns. He began his pro career in 1985 with the San Francisco 49ers and retired in 2004 with the Seattle Seahawks. Rice has played in 13 Pro Bowl games and won 3 Super Bowls.

21. UCLA holds 11 NCAA titles. The Bruins have won 23 of their last 41 league titles and have been in the NCAA playoffs for 35 of the last 41 years.

22. The St. Louis Blues play at the Savvis Center, which holds 21,000 fans. The 664,000-square-foot Savvis Center can also hold nearly 22,000 for basketball, concerts and other floor-seating events.

23. Pete Sampras has won 14 grand slam titles. He has won 2 Australian Opens, 7 Wimbledon titles, and 5 U.S. Opens.

24. A total of 20 horses run in the Kentucky Derby. There are about

ANSWERS

35,000 three-year-old thoroughbred horses in the world, and some 400 owners nominate their horses for the Derby each year.

25. Ty Cobb had the highest career batting average with .367. He also holds the record for the most career batting titles (12) and the most career steals of home plate.

26. John Stockon has 3,265 career steals. Stockton played as a point guard for the Utah Jazz during his entire career from 1984 to 2003. He also won two gold medals as part of the Olympic basketball team in 1992 and 1996.

27. On two different occasions, players kicked field goals that sailed 63 yards—Tom Dempsey, New Orleans Saints vs. Detroit Lions, Nov. 8, 1970; Jason Elam, Denver Broncos vs. Jacksonville Jaguars, Oct. 25, 1998.

28. Wayne Gretzky has 2,857 points in the NHL. He scored 894 goals during his 20-year career. He became the first person in the league to average more than 2 points per game.

29. The athletes of Norway have won a total of 263 medals at the Winter Olympics—94 gold medals, 94 silver medals, and 75 bronze medals.

30. Nolan Ryan had 5,714 strikeouts during his career. Nicknamed "The Ryan Express," he played for 27 seasons and is considered one of the greatest pitchers to have ever played.

31. Wilt Chamberlain has 23,924 career rebounds. He also holds the career record for the most rebounds in one game (55), and the seasonal record for the most rebounds per game (27).

32. Steve Young has a quarterback rating of 96.8. He began his NFL career with the Tampa Bay Buccaneers in 1985 and retired with the San Francisco 49ers in 1999. Young was the first left-handed quarterback to be inducted into the Pro Football Hall of Fame.

33. Tennessee holds 6 NCAA titles. The Lady Vols' latest win came in 1998—the same year they had a perfect 39-0 record. This was the most seasonal wins ever recorded for a women's basketball team.

34. Bobby Hull rocketed a slap shot that was recorded at 118.3 mph. Hull played from 1957–1972, and then from 1979–1980. He led the league in scoring three times (1960, 1962, 1966) and was voted league MVP in 1965 and 1966.

41. Shaun Alexander scored 28 touchdowns during the 2005 season. He scored the record-making touchdown on January 1, 2006 in a game against the Green Bay Packers.

35. Cy Young lost 316 games during his MLB career. Young started in the major leagues in 1890 with the Cleveland Spiders and won 511 games during his career—a record that still stands today.

36. With a scoring average of 30.12, Michael Jordan holds the NBA record for highest scoring average. He is narrowly ahead of Wilt Chamberlain, whose scoring average is 30.06.

37. Jerry Rice has 1,549 career receptions. His career receiving yards total 22,895. He led the NFL in receiving and touchdown receptions for 6 of his 20 seasons.

38. With 2,219 medals, the athletes of the United States have dominated the Summer Olympics. They have won 907 gold medals, 697 silver medals, and 615 bronze medals.

39. Soccer is played by approximately 20 million people in more than 140 countries throughout the world.

40. Mark Price has a free throw average of .904, having attempted 2,362 shots and making 2,135 of them. He also has an average of 40% for three-point shots and more than 50% for shots from the field.

42. The Boston Celtics have won 16 NBA Championships between 1857 and 1986. The have also won 19 conference titles and 25 division titles.

ANSWERS

1. There are more than 1 million types of insects throughout the world. There are about 91,000 different species of insects in the United States alone.

2. A group of toads is called a knot. There are approximately 200 species of toads throughout the world, and these nocturnal hunters are poisonous to predators.

3. A hummingbird is the only animal that can fly backward. It can move each wing in a circle, similar to a helicopter. This motion also allows the hummingbird to hover, move side to side, and fly straight up and down.

4. A caged mouse will run approximately 2.5 miles each night on an exercise wheel.

5. The Komodo dragon can eat equal to 80% of its body weight at one time. This giant lizard weighs about 300 pounds, so this means its meal can be about 240 pounds.

6. A flea can jump 350 times its body length in one leap. That's the equivalent of a human jumping the length of a football field.

7. The venom in one bite from a black mamba snake can kill up to 200 humans. This 14-foot-long snake is a member of the cobra family and is very aggressive.

8. A bat can eat as many as 1,200 insects in one hour while it is feeding each night. Bats use a special kind of sonar called echolocation to find all of these tasty treats.

9. A male saltwater crocodile can reach a length of 22 feet. These crocodiles live in Australia and the East Indies. They are also known as estuarine crocodiles and Indo-Pacific crocodiles.

10. A grasshopper has five eyes. Two large compound eyes are located on each side of its head. One single eye is above the base of each antenna, and another is mid-way between the two antennae.

11. An eagle's nest is called an aerie. It can measure 8 feet in diameter, 16 feet in depth, and can weigh up to 4,000 pounds.

12. There are approximately 30,000 different lenses making up a dragonfly's eye. In comparison, a human eye has just one lens.

13. A cheetah can run at a top speed of 65 miles per hour. Found in eastern and southwestern Africa, these powerful cats will chase their prey for about 60 seconds with a 50% success rate.

14. There are more than 400,000 known types of beetles in the world. Beetles account for about 40% of all insects. One in every five animals on the planet is a beetle.

15. There are 220 million olfactory receptors on a dog's nose—about 40 times the number in a human's nose. With that kind of sniffer, some dogs can smell scents up to a half mile away.

16. A male duck is called a drake. Male ducks have bright feathers and colorful markings to attract females.

17. A giant squid's eye can measure about 11 inches in diameter—about the same size as a dinner plate. The giant eyes can also focus independently, allowing the squid to see in two different directions.

18. Blowflies have about 3,000 hairs on their feet, which they use to taste their food. Their feet are about 10 million times more sensitive than the human tongue.

19. A group of rabbits is called a nest. A litter of young usually consists of 3 to 4 bunnies, and a female rabbit has between 4 to 6 litters each year.

20. A queen termite can lay about 40,000 eggs in one day, and it takes about two weeks for eggs to hatch. Depending on the type of termite, a colony may contain between 10,000 and 370,000 termites.

21. A camel can drink 30 gallons in just 10 minutes. That equals 320 cans of soda.

22. A male peacock has 200 long feathers on his back. The tail, also known as a train, helps the peacock attract a mate. The large tail is also used to frighten enemies.

23. John Quincy Adams had an alligator as a pet. The reptile was a gift from the Marquis de Lafayette in 1826, and it lived in the White House for several months.

ANSWERS

24. There are approximately 165,000 Labrador Retrievers registered in the United States. This breed has been the top dog in U.S. homes for 16 consecutive years.

25. There are about 1,075 species currently considered endangered or threatened. Approximately 340 of these are mammals, some 275 are birds, about 125 are fish, and another 115 are reptiles.

26. It takes 24 chicken eggs to equal the volume of one ostrich egg. An ostrich egg can weigh about 4 pounds and can measure 5 inches by 6 inches.

27. A jellyfish is made up of 95% water. There are about 2,000 species of jellyfish, and none have heads or hearts. A simple lifeform, these spineless creatures have been on the planet for about 650 million years.

28. A hummingbird may visit about 2,000 flowers in one day. With each visit, they collect the flower's nectar for food. At the same time, they help the plant to pollinate.

29. Approximately 50,000 bees can live in a hive at one time. The colony can visit plants that cover about 40 square miles, and will collect about 260 pounds of nectar a year.

30. A koala sleeps for about 22 hours a day. Koalas are nocturnal, waking at night to feed on eucalyptus leaves.

31. An ichthyologist studies the anatomy, behavior, conservation, and history of the 25,000 to 30,000 known species of bony fish, sharks, and rays.

32. A kangaroo can cover about 30 feet in one leap. These marsupials are from Australia and can hop along at a speed of 40 miles per hour.

33. Monarch butterflies can travel up to 1,800 miles each year. The United States' Monarch population spends the summer in the northern part of the country, and then migrates to Florida, Texas, or Mexico.

34. Chameleons can move their eyes in two different directions. Each eye can focus separately, allowing the chameleon to see potential prey approaching from any direction.

35. A giraffe's tongue can measure 18 inches in length. A male giraffe can grow to 19 feet tall and weigh about 3,000 pounds.

36. There are approximately 25,000 Persian cats registered in the United States. It has been the most popular cat breed in the country since 1871.

37. A cockroach can live without a head for about 14 days. The insect does not use its head to breathe, and it can go without eating for almost a month.

38. A baby swan is called a cygnet. It is born with gray fuzz covering its body and doesn't look like its parents. During the next year, the cygnet will molt, and new white feathers will grow in.

39. A slug has four noses. A slug is a type of mollusk similar to a snail, but without a shell.

40. The pouch of a pelican's beak can hold 3 gallons of water at one time. This expandable sac of skin is used as a net to scoop fish out of the water.

41. A cat has 32 muscles in each ear. These muscles help a cat rotate its ears independently some 180 degrees. In comparison, a human has just 6 ear muscles.

42. A chicken will fully develop and hatch from an egg in 21 days. In the United States, some 90 billion eggs were produced in 2005.

ANSWERS

PAGES 46–59

1. Stevie Wonder has won 21 Grammies during his career. Wonder has also scored 30 top-ten hits, as well as a lifetime achievement award and an Oscar for Best Song.

2. *Sledgehammer* by Peter Gabriel is the most-aired video on MTV. The hit song was released in 1986 off the album *So*. In 1987, the video won a record 9 MTV Video Music Awards.

3. *Titanic* has grossed $1.83 billion worldwide since it opened in 1997. The James Cameron blockbuster drama starred Leonardo DiCaprio and Kate Winslet, and won a record 11 Academy Awards.

4. There are 232 puppets used during Disney's *The Lion King*. The play opened in 1997 and is currently produced at the Minskoff Theater in New York City. The play has won 6 Tony Awards, including Best Musical.

5. The now-famous numbers from *Lost* include 4, 8, 15, 16, 23, and 42. They were lucky for Hurley, who used them to win the lottery, but not so lucky for the thousands of actual people who have played them in hopes of winning the lottery across the country.

6. *The Phantom of the Opera* has been performed more than 7,701 times since it opened in 1986. It is estimated that the show has been seen by 80 million people worldwide with ticket sales totaling $3.2 billion.

7. Some 81% of Americans watch television at least once a day. About 57% of those viewers watch the tube for less than two hours, while 7% of them watch for more than five hours.

8. Boston Rob Mariano did not win the grand prize on either *Survivor* season he competed in. His first appearance on the reality series was on *Survivor Marquesas*, where he was voted off seventh. He later appeared on the "Survivor All Stars" competition, where he came in second.

9. Country is the most popular radio format in the United States, with more than 2,050 stations from coast to coast.

Country music stations are generally divided into two categories—classic country and hot country.

10. During the first weekend of July in 2006, *Pirates of the Caribbean: Dead Man's Chest* grossed $135.6 million in 4,133 theaters. The film stars Johnny Depp, Orlando Bloom, and Keira Knightly.

11. The Rolling Stones earned $162 million in 2005, mostly due to their *A Bigger Bang* tour. The average ticket price was $133.98. The tour sold approximately 1.2 million tickets.

12. David Letterman earned $40 million in 2005. *Late Night with David Letterman* debuted on NBC in 1982. Letterman later switched to the CBS network and has been on *The Late Show with David Letterman* ever since.

13. *E.T.* spent 16 consecutive weekends at number one. The film was released on June 11, 1982 and has grossed more than $792 million worldwide.

14. The Simpsons reside on 714 Evergreen Terrace. *The Simpsons* became the longest-running prime time animated show in 1997. Some of the celebrities that have appeared on the show include Drew Barrymore, Michael Jackson, Blink 182, and Willie Nelson.

15. *Harry Potter and the Sorcerer's Stone*—the first movie in the series—has grossed $974.6 million

worldwide since it opened in 2001. It is the third-highest-grossing movie of all time.

16. Dopey is the only one of the seven dwarfs that does not have a beard. Dopey is also the only dwarf that has never spoken a word on film.

17. Billy Joel's *52nd Street* was the first CD ever manufactured when it was made in 1982. The album featured the hits "Big Shot," "My Life," and "Honesty."

18. Animated sensation *Shrek 2* has grossed more than $440 million since it opened in May 2004. Diaz provided the voice for Princess Fiona.

19 The Fresh Prince—also known as Will Smith—and DJ Jazzy Jeff won the first ever Grammy for a rap performance in 1989. They won the award for the song "Parents Just Don't Understand."

20. Alecia Moore—better known as Pink—has released three albums since she burst onto the music scene in 2000. Some of her most well-known songs include "Don't Let Me Get Me," "Get the Party Started," and "Family Portrait."

26. Barbra Streisand has 43 solo albums that have achieved gold album award status. She also has seven albums that she released with other artists that have also gone gold. With these 50 gold albums, she is second in the all-time charts behind Elvis Presley.

21. In October 1975, Bruce Springsteen appeared on the covers of both *Newsweek* and *Time*. Both magazines were recognizing the success of his album "Born to Run," which included songs about surviving and rising above difficult times.

22. Jennifer Lopez's romantic comedy *The Wedding Planner*, and her hot album *J. Lo* both hit number one on the same weekend in January 2001. *The Wedding Planner* went on to gross $94.7 million, and *J. Lo* stayed in the top twenty albums chart for six weeks.

23. Approximately 43,000 sketches were drawn for *Cars* by the film's animators. Once a sketch is complete, it can take up to six months for it to be turned into the computer version seen in the movie.

24. LeAnn Rimes was just 14 years old when she won her first Grammy Award for Best New Artist in 1997. Some of Rimes' most popular songs include "How Do I Live?," "I Need You," and "Blue."

25. Comedian Chris Rock does the voice for Marty the Zebra in the 2005 animated hit *Madagascar*. Marty is the adventurous one of his pals and wants to see what life is like outside of the zoo.

27. Jim Carrey's *How the Grinch Stole Christmas* earned more than $260 million since it opened in November 2000 and is the star's most profitable movie.

28. Rory and Lorelai live in Stars Hollow, Connecticut. The town is actually a Warner Brothers backlot set originally used for the 1946 film *Saratoga Trunk*.

29. Billy Joel became the first singer to appear in concert at Yankee Stadium when he appeared in front of a sold-out crowd in June 1990. After that, U2 and Pink Floyd also played at the stadium.

30. Out of Tom Cruise's 31 movies, a total of 15 of them have earned more than $100 million. Some of his most profitable movies include *Mission: Impossible*, *The War of the Worlds*, *The Last Samurai*, and *Mission: Impossible 2*.

31. It costs $250 to buy a vowel on *Wheel of Fortune*. Even if the vowel is not in the puzzle, the contestant still loses the $250.

If there is more than one vowel in the puzzle, the contestant is only charged once.

32. Mariah Carey saw her first 5 singles shoot to number one on the *Billboard* Hot 100 chart. These singles included "Vision Of Love," "Someday," "Love Takes Time," "I Don't Want To Cry," and "Emotions."

33. Supermodel Gisele Bundchen earns about $30 million a year, mostly through her 20 different fashion contracts. Some of these profitable gigs include Victoria's Secret, Dolce & Gabbana, and Ebel watches.

34. *Superman Returns* opened in June 2006 with a budget of $204 million. The film stars Brandon Routh as Superman, Kevin Spacey as Lex Luthor, and Kate Bosworth as Lois Lane.

35. SpongeBob SquarePants calls Bikini Bottom home. He lives there in a pineapple under the sea, and works at The Krusty Krab.

36. C-3PO is the first character to speak in *Star Wars*. Anthony Daniels supplied the voice for the interpreter droid.

37. Donald Duck's middle name is Fauntleroy. It was shown once in a wartime cartoon. Donald debuted in 1934, and there have been 128 cartoons written about him since then.

38. A 30-second commercial that aired during Super Bowl XL cost a whopping $2.5 million—about $100,000 more than the year before. This set a record high for advertising during the big game.

39. Celine Dion has sold more than 175 million albums worldwide. The Canadian singer's first album came in 1990, and she has gone on to win several Grammy Awards.

40. Even though Elvis Presley died in August 1977, he still continues to earn more than some of today's hottest celebrities. The money is generated by music sales, re-released movies and songs, Graceland visits, and documentaries.

41. *Star Wars: Episode III - Revenge of the Sith* earned an impressive $380.2 million in 2005. It opened on May 19 and went on to play in 3,661 theaters before it closed on October 20.

42. Best Animal Performance has never been a category at the MTV Movie Awards. The award show began in 1992, and the winners are chosen by the public.

ANSWERS

1. All the nerves of the human body would combine to stretch some 47 miles! The nervous system is the most complex system of the body.

2. The adult human brain weighs 3 pounds. This is about 2% of a person's total body weight. The brain measures about 5.5 inches wide and 6.6 inches long.

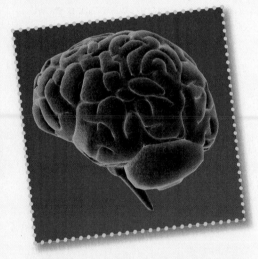

3. There are 5 million hairs on the human body. That's about the same number as a full-grown gorilla. However, a human's hair is thin and small, and is sometimes hard to see.

4. There are 1,500 miles of airways located in the lungs. And they are packed in pretty tight, considering each lung measures between 10 to 12 inches long.

5. The muscles in the eye are the busiest muscles in the body. They move more than 100,000 times each day.

6. Each minute, kids take an average of 20 breaths. When you breathe in, your lungs fill with oxygen. When you breathe out, your lungs push out carbon dioxide.

7. The thigh bone, or femur, is the longest bone in the body. It can be about one-fourth your total height.

8. If a human nose is in peak performance, it can tell the difference between 10,000 different smells. However, sense of smell lessens with age, and a child is much more likely to distinguish between smells than an adult is.

9. You shed about 40 pounds of skin in a lifetime. Shed skin cells contribute to household dust, and are the favorite food of dust mites.

10. Some 440 gallons of blood flow through the kidneys each day. The kidneys filter out about 2 quarts of waste and water daily.

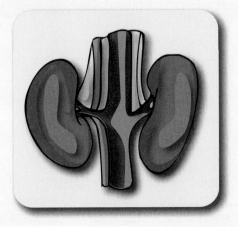

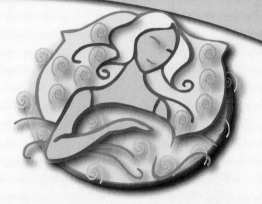

11. The brain is 85% water. It uses 20% of the body's oxygen supply and 20% of the body's blood supply.

12. The hyoid bone is the only bone in the body not connected to another. The v-shaped bone is located at the base of the tongue to support it.

13. It takes 47 muscles to frown. On the flip side, it takes only 17 muscles to smile.

14. The average man has 5 to 6 liters of blood circulating through his body. As the blood circulates, it carries nutrients and oxygen to the cells in the body.

15. There are 27 bones in the human hand. They are divided into three groups, including the carpal bones in the wrist, the metacarpal bones in the knuckles, and the phalange bones.

16. The average adult had 32 teeth in his or her mouth. Adult teeth start to come in at five or six years, and are usually all in by the age of 20.

17. An adult has about 5 dreams a night. Most dreams occur in the REM—or deepest stage—of sleep, which occurs every 90 minutes or so.

18. The liver is the largest solid organ in the body. The stomach and intestines are the largest hollow organs in the body.

19. The average person produces 10,000 gallons of saliva in a lifetime. That's the equivalent of 106,667 cans of soda.

20. An adult's blood circulates through the body 1,500 times a day. That's more than 62 times an hour.

21. About 10% of your body weight is your blood. If you divide your weight by 12, that will tell you the approximate number of pints of blood in your body.

22. The heart beats about 100,000 times a day. That averages about 35 million times a year and 2.5 billion times during a lifetime.

ANSWERS

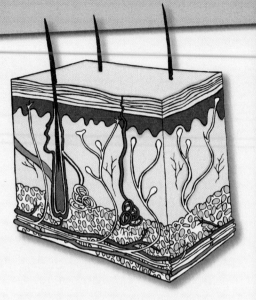

23. The aorta leading into the heart is the largest artery in the body. It is the same width as a garden hose. A capillary, however, is very tiny. It takes about ten of them to equal the width of a human hair.

24. All the blood vessels in an adult's body would circle the Earth 2.5 times! There are more than 60,000 miles of vessels in a child's body and close to 100,000 miles of vessels in an adult's body.

25. A person loses about 80 hairs each day. There are approximately 300,000 hairs on the scalp, and the hair grows approximately half an inch each month.

26. There are approximately 1 trillion cells in an adult's body.

27. There are 206 bones in an adult's body. Babies are actually born with more than 300 bones, but many fuse together as the child grows.

28. An adult has 20 square feet of skin. That's about the same size as a blanket. All together, an adult's skin weighs about 9 pounds.

29. The hardest substance in the body is enamel found on the teeth. The defensive coating helps to protect the soft insides of the tooth.

30. An adult's stomach can hold about 1.5 liters—or just more than 6 cups. The stomach will also produce about 2 liters of hydrochloric acid daily to dissolve this material.

31. The liver performs more than 500 functions. Some of the most important include regulating substances in your body, storing vital nutrients, and purifying waste and toxins.

32. The stirrup—a tiny bone in the inner ear—is the smallest bone in the human body. It can measure just one-tenth of an inch.

33. A cough can reach a top speed of 60 miles an hour. A sneeze can reach a top speed of 100 miles per hour.

34. Your sense of smell is worst in the morning. It gets better as the day goes on. The human nose uses some 12 million olfactory receptor cells to detect scents.

35. The small intestine is 22 feet in length, which is actually larger than the large intestine. However, it is only 1 to 2 inches around. The large intestine is just 5 feet long, but measures 3 to 4 inches around.

36. It takes about 6 months for a fingernail to grow from base to tip. Fingernails grow faster than toenails.

37. Beards are the fastest-growing hairs on the body. If a man never cut his beard, it could grow up to 30 feet long during his lifetime.

38. There are approximately 32 million bacteria on every square inch of the body. The most common places to find bacteria are moist areas, including armpits and between the toes.

39. The heart pumps about 300 quarts of blood during a lifetime. That's enough blood to fill more than 3 super tanker trucks.

40. The lungs are the only organ that can float on water. This is because lungs are mostly made up of little pockets of air.

41. There are approximately 10,000 taste buds in an adult's mouth. Most of these get replaced every two weeks. However, as a person ages, fewer taste buds get replaced and the sense of taste diminishes.

42. A person blinks about 17,280 times a day. All of this blinking serves two purposes—to keep eyes moist, and to keep dust and other objects out of the eyes.

ANSWERS

PAGES 74–87

1. In the United States, the odds of giving birth to twins are about 3% (1 in 33). The states with the highest number of twins born are Connecticut and Massachusetts.

2. Some 850,000 kids—or 2% of the population of students ages 5 to 17—are homeschooled.

3. The odds of dying from a lightning strike are 1 in 71,500. That means that 1 person out of every 71,500 people will die from a lightning strike. About 84% of those victims are male.

4. More than 70% of dog owners buy Christmas presents for their pooches.

5. The odds of being hit by an asteroid from space are about 1 in 200,000.

6. One in every 563 people at a MLB baseball game will catch a foul ball from the stands. About 50 balls are used in each game, and the average attendance at a game is 28,000.

7. A person has a 1 in 10 million shot at becoming the President of the United States. The average president is between 40 to 72 years old. So, a person has about 8 chances in his or her lifetime since a president is elected every four years.

8. Just 1 in every 6 million people will be attacked by a shark during a lifetime in the United States. There are less than 50 serious shark attacks in the country each year.

9. Only 12% of the students who apply to Harvard actually get accepted. The average SAT scores of the accepted students range from 1,380 to 1,570.

10. Just 12% of public elementary schools reported selling soda in 2005. Only 2% of the schools sell it in the cafeteria.

11. About 48% of children ages 4 through 12 have televisions in their bedrooms. Another 24% of toddlers and 60% of teens have televisions in their rooms.

12. A person will have to search through about 10,000 clovers before they find one with four leaves.

13. Some 52% of Americans pick chocolate ice cream. Berry and vanilla flavors are tied for second place.

17. According to Kodak, approximately 4% of all the amateur photos snapped in the world take place at Walt Disney World.

18. Silver cars—the most popular color for the last 5 years—make up 26% of all the automobiles on the road. The second most popular color is white with 16%, followed by red with 14%.

19. Each year, rock music accounts for about 24% of all CD and cassette music sales. Country is the second most popular with 13%.

20. About 46% of all American homes have three or more television sets. More than 107 million homes have at least one set.

21. Some 59% of kids ages 6 to 17 participate either in after school sports, clubs, or lessons.

14. About 82% of the kids in America dress up for Halloween. And adults are joining in the fun too, with 67% of them wearing some type of costume.

15. American internet users make up 18% of the world's web surfers. There are almost 200 million internet users in the country today.

16. For every 220 books that are published, just one will reach the *New York Times* bestsellers list. There are 35 bestsellers each week, and only about 15% of those are fiction.

22. Since the pageant began in 1921, some 7% of the winners have been from California. The two other highly successful states include Pennsylvania and Ohio with 6% each.

ANSWERS

26. Video games are currently the most popular type of toy, accounting for 28% of the market. Toys for preschoolers are the second highest in sales.

27. About 71% of Americans rent a movie or pay to watch one in their homes each week.

28. Although many people assume the odds of having a baby girl is 50%, it is actually only about 48.8%. There are about 1,048 boys born for every 1,000 girls.

23. The United States accounts for 29% of all launches, which includes about 1,490 missions. The leader—Russia—holds the record with 39% of the launches.

24. Some 63% of families keep the television on while they are eating dinner.

25. With more than 400,000 people working in fields that qualify for Academy Awards, and only some 38 Oscars given out each year, just 1 in 11,500 will actually win an award.

29. Approximately 23% of Americans think the penny is no longer useful.

30. When it comes to working out, about 67% of Americans claim to do it at least once a week. Another 24% say they exercise every few months.

31. An American spends about 32% of his or her day in front of the tube. This includes time spent actively watching the set, and having it on while doing other things.

32. Just 20% of all registered climbers will reach the summit of Mount Everest. In the last 85 years, only about 1,300 people have been successful.

33. Almost a quarter of all holiday shoppers—some 23%—wait until the last minute to do their shopping.

34. About 14% of adults in the United States do some kind of charity work.

35. A PGA golfer sinks a hole in one for every 2,491 shots he makes. During one year, about 33 holes in one are scored on the PGA Tour.

36. Only 5% of American households own birds. That's about 15 million households with feathered friends.

37. Kids aged 14 years and younger account for 50% of all sneaker sales in the United States.

38. About 20% of all American adults read books two or more times a week. That's about 60 million people.

39. Some 18% of advertising is done in the newspaper. About 85% of it is done in local papers, and the rest is done in national papers.

40. About 32% of the families in the United States barbecue at least once a summer.

41. For every 22,000 U.S. citizens, just one becomes a professional athlete. The hardest league to break into is the NBA, taking only 1 athlete in 3,300. MLB, however, picks 1 in every 250 players.

42. More than three-quarters of U.S. homes—or 76%—own at least one DVD player.

ANSWERS

1. The Sun's light reaches Earth in about 8.3 minutes. The light travels at 186,282 miles per second.

2. NASA stands for National Aeronautics and Space Administration. NASA was formed in 1958 to further aerospace exploration and to make breakthroughs in general science and technology.

3. Blue stars are the hottest. They have surface temperatures of about 30,000 degrees Fahrenheit. Red stars are about 3,000 degrees Fahrenheit. Yellow stars have surface temperatures of 6,000 degrees Fahrenheit.

4. There are 88 different constellations, or patterns of stars, in the sky. These constellations are often associated with mythology.

5. Water will freeze when it reaches a temperature of 32°F.

6. The Earth's plates move very slowly, covering about 2.2 inches each year. The Earth's crust is made up of about 20 different plates that vary in size.

7. The Mariana Trench is the deepest part of the ocean floor. It measures 36,197.5 feet deep and is located in the Pacific Ocean off the coast of Japan.

8. The tides in the Bay of Fundy can vary by up to 55 feet. The bay is located off the northern coast of Maine and extends into Canada between New Brunswick and Nova Scotia.

9. Oxygen is the most common element in the Earth's crust, accounting for almost half of it. The second most-common elements are silica (28%) and aluminum (8%).

10. There are more than 100 billion stars in the Milky Way galaxy.

11. A bolt of lightning is about 54,000°F. Lightning can travel at speeds up to 93,000 miles per second and will heat the air it passes through in a millionth of a second.

12. The hottest temperature ever recorded was 136°F in Libya in 1922. Death Valley in California is a close second with a top temperature of 134°F in 1913.

13. The coldest temperature ever recorded on Earth was -128.6°F in Antarctica in 1983. About 98% of the area is covered with snow and ice, which reflects the sun's rays instead of absorbing them.

14. The longest range is the Andes of South America. The Andes measure 4,700 miles long and were created when two of the Earth's plates collided.

15. Teddy bears are not allowed in space because they give off atoms of gas very easily. This would create problems with the pressure within the shuttle cabin.

16. Scientists estimate that there are approximately 500,000 detectable earthquakes in the world annually. About 100,000 of those can be felt, and 100 of them cause damage.

17. Some 36% of Americans' trash is made up of paper products and cardboard. The second most-common item is yard waste at 20%.

18. It takes just eight minutes for the shuttle to fly at 17,000 miles per hour. Each of the solid rocket boosters on a Space Shuttle contains more than one million pounds of propellant.

19. Saudi Arabia has the greatest oil reserves in the world with 264 billion barrels. The runner up is Canada with 179 billion barrels.

20. More than 70 inches of rain fall in a rain forest each year. The world's rain forests are located in Asia, Africa, South America, Central America, and on the Pacific islands.

United States

ANSWERS

21. Two molecules of hydrogen and one molecule of oxygen combine to make water. Water has the chemical formula H_2O.

22. An agronomist studies soil and agriculture. He or she researches ways to produce crops and manage soils to benefit the environment.

23. The asteroid belt is located between Mars and Jupiter. Most of the asteroids in the solar system are in orbit there.

24. A tornado's winds can reach speeds of 300 miles per hour. The diameter of a tornado's funnel cloud can vary from just a few feet to more than a mile.

25. Between 1998 and 1999, Mount Baker, Washington, recorded 1,140 inches of snow. That's 95 feet—taller than a 9-story building.

26. There are 250,000 different types of flowering plants in the world. This includes almost 600 species of carnivorous plants that capture and kill insects for their nutrients.

27. The astronauts of *Apollo 11* landed on the Moon on July 20, 1969. During this mission, Neil Armstrong and Buzz Aldrin became the first humans to land on the moon.

28. A bristlecone pine in Wheeler Peak, Nevada, is more than 4,600 years old. Bristlecone pines grow very slowly, and their dense wood is resistant to insects and disease.

29. The Earth moves around the Sun at a speed of 67,000 miles per hour. Even at that speed, it takes the Earth 365 days to completely orbit the Sun.

30. The flower of a Rafflesia can reach 3 feet in diameter and weigh 15 pounds. It is also called the stinking corpse lily because of its terrible smell.

31. About 97% of the world's water is located in the oceans. The surface area of all of the oceans combined is 139.5 million square miles.

32. Some 7% of the Earth is covered with tropical rain forest. The trees help to remove carbon dioxide from the air as they supply oxygen.

33. There are 9 million cubic miles of ice in the world. Most of this ice is located at the south pole.

34. There are about 1,500 active volcanoes that have erupted in the last 10,000 years located around the world.

35. Dinosaurs roamed the Earth during the Mesozoic era. The Mesozoic era lasted about 180 million years, and includes the Triassic, Jurassic, and Cretaceous periods.

36. In November of 1957, a Russian dog named Laika was launched into space. She traveled on the Soviet spacecraft the *Sputnik 2.*

37. An astronaut's space suit does not come equipped with chewing gum. The life raft and parachute are included as safety precautions.

38. Nitrogen makes up 78% of the atmosphere. Nitrogen was discovered in 1772 by Daniel Rutherford.

39. About 30 acres of rain forests are destroyed each minute. Many trees are cut down for firewood and building materials, and a great deal of land has been cleared for farmland.

40. Saturn's rings are made up of ice, dust, and rock. This debris varies in size from a grain of sand to a tall building.

41. Alaska is the most earthquake-prone state, experiencing at least one major magnitude-7 quake each year.

42. It takes 30 million trees to create all of the newspapers in the United States annually. However, recycling one ton of paper saves one acre of trees.

ANSWERS

PAGES 102–115

1. Russia is the largest country in the world, measuring 6,591,027 square miles. Canada is the second-largest country with 3,854,082 square miles.

2. Vatican City measures just 0.2 square miles and is completely surrounded by Rome, Italy.

3. Mount Everest is located in Tibet. The great mountain measures 29,035 feet tall and was formed about 60 million years ago.

4. With 125,567 miles of coastline, Canada is number one.

5. The Pacific Ocean is the largest body of water and covers more than 64.1 million square miles.

6. Andorra has a life expectancy of 83.5 years. The small European country has a population on about 71,000 and is mostly made up of Spanish and Andorran people.

7. With more than 840,000 square miles, Greenland is the world's largest island. That's more than the next three largest islands combined.

8. Angel Falls is located in Venezuela and measures 3,212 feet tall. It is located on the Carrao River in South America.

9. The Nile is the longest River in the World. It measures 4,158 miles long and flows through Burundi, Democratic Republic of Congo, Egypt, Eritrea, Ethiopia, Kenya, Rwanda, Sudan, Tanzania, and Uganda.

10. Uganda has the world's youngest population with just over half the citizens under the age of 15. The country has a high birth rate, as well as a high death rate.

11. China is the world's most populated country with 1.3 billion people. That's more than one-sixth of the entire world population. India is second with 1.1 billion.

12. Tokyo, Japan, is the largest capital city in the world with 34.4 million people. It accounts for about 27% of Japan's population and is expected to grow about 5% by 2015.

13. Asia is the world's largest continent, accounting for about 21.4% of Earth. It is 11.9 million square miles and holds more than 60% of the world's population.

14. Tuvalu has the smallest population in the world with just 11,600 people.

15. The Sahara is located in northern Africa. It measures 3.5 million square miles.

16. France is the top tourist country with more than 75 million visitors each year. Spain is second with 53.6 million.

17. There are more than 874 million people who speak Mandarin Chinese throughout the world.

18. With about 23% of the population older than sixty-five years of age, Monaco claims the world's oldest population.

19. China has the longest border at 13,761 miles. Russia is second with a border measuring 12,403 miles long.

20. Russia has the most forested area. More than 3.3 million square miles are covered by trees and bushes.

ANSWERS

21. A total of 21 states end in the letter A. They are Alabama, Alaska, Arizona, California, Florida, Georgia, Indiana, Iowa, Louisiana, Minnesota, Montana, Nebraska, Nevada, North Carolina, North Dakota, Oklahoma, Pennsylvania, South Carolina, South Dakota, Virginia, West Virginia.

22. The United States has the most marriages in the world with more than 2.3 million each year.

23. China and Russia each border 14 neighboring countries. China borders Afghanistan, Bhutan, India, Kazakhstan, Kyrgyzstan, Laos, Mongolia, Myanmar, Nepal, North Korea, Pakistan, Russia, Tajikistan, and Vietnam. Russia borders Azerbaijan, Belarus, China, Estonia, Finland, Georgia, Kazakhstan, Latvia, Lithuania, Mongolia, North Korea, Norway, Poland, and Ukraine.

24. The people of Switzerland eat more than 25 pounds of chocolate every year. Ireland is second with 24 pounds, and the UK is third with 22 pounds.

25. The are currently 193 countries in the world. The world's newest country is Montenegro which split from Serbia in June 2006.

26. Djibouti, a small country in Africa, is entirely a desert. Less than 1 square mile is suitable for farming.

27. A total of 57 countries list English as their official language. The next most-common official language is French, which is used by 33 countries.

28. There are 57.5 million square miles of land on earth. There are also 139.4 million square miles of water on earth.

29. Japan's *Yomiuri Shimbun* has the highest average daily circulation with 14.3 million readers. In fact, the top five most-read newspapers in the world are all from Japan.

30. With more than 200 million users online, the United States dominates the Internet. China is next with 120 million users, followed by Japan with 87 million users.

31. Ojos del Salado in Chile is the world's tallest volcano at 22,595 feet. It is located in the Atacama Desert in South America.

32. Luxembourg has the most cell phone users with 106.1 users per 100 people. This means that many people have more than one cell phone.

33. The world's largest library is the Library of Congress, located in Washington, DC. It contains more than 29 million books.

34. Although it is not actually called a lake, the Caspian Sea has an area of 152,239 square miles. The lake borders Azerbaijan, Russia, Kazakhstan, Turkmenistan, and Iran.

35. Mammoth Cave in central Kentucky has more than 345 miles of tunnels. The cave area measures about 10 miles in diameter.

36. The average years spent in school for each person in Norway is 16.9. The second most-educated country is Finland with an average of 16.7 years, followed by Australia with 16.6 years.

37. Each person in Luxembourg donates an average of $496.59 to charity per year. The second most-generous country is Denmark with each citizen donating approximately $366.93 annually.

38. A whopping 98% of Antarctica is covered by thick sheets of ice. That's about 7 million cubic miles of ice—or 90% of the world's total.

39. Vatican City—the world's smallest country—mails an average of 7,200 pieces of mail per person annually.

40. The Dead Sea in the country of Jordan on the Asian continent is the lowest point on Earth. The sea is more than 1,349 feet below sea level.

41. The people of Thailand watch the most television—more than 22 hours each week.

42. North America measures about 9.4 million square miles and is the third-largest continent. Made up of Canada, the United States, and Mexico, North America holds about 365 million people.

ANSWERS

PAGES 116–129

1. Mr. Potato Head was the first toy advertised on television. In 1952, the ad used the slogan, "Meet Mr. Potato Head, the most wonderful friend a boy or girl could have!"

2. Some 5.1 million pounds of sheet metal are used annually to make Tonka trucks. They also use 119,000 pounds of yellow paint to coat all of these trucks.

3. There are three Barbie Dolls sold each second.

4. Binny & Smith produces 20,000 Silly Putty eggs each day. That totals about 1,500 pounds of putty per day.

5. Some 147,000 words can be used. Scrabble was invented by Alfred Mosher Butts, an out-of-work architect, and was first trademarked in 1948.

6. The Corvette is the bestselling Hot Wheels vehicle. In total, more than 1,000 different types of vehicles have been created in the last 39 years.

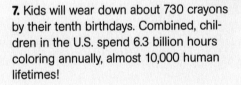

7. Kids will wear down about 730 crayons by their tenth birthdays. Combined, children in the U.S. spend 6.3 billion hours coloring annually, almost 10,000 human lifetimes!

8. Play-Doh was originally introduced as a wallpaper cleaner in 1950. If all the Play-Doh sold since then were rolled into a rope, it would stretch around the world 300 times.

9. It takes just 10 seconds to produce one Slinky.

10. The yo-yo was first used in Greece more than 3,000 years ago.

11. The first jigsaw puzzle was made by a mapmaker in 1767 and showed a map of the world.

12. Madame Alexander invented "sleep eyes" for dolls in the 1930s. When the dolls are tilted backward, their eyes close.

13. The U.S. toy industry averages about $21 billion in sales annually. Mass marketers and discount stores account for about half of all toy sales, while toy stores make up less than 25% of total revenue.

14. If all the Playmobil figures ever made were lined up end-to-end, they would circle Earth one and a half times.

15. More than 30 million Trivial Pursuit games have been sold worldwide. They are available in 18 languages throughout 32 countries. Some of the more current popular versions of the game include Trivial Pursuit For Kids Volume 6, Trivial Pursuit Book Lover's Edition, and the Trivial Pursuit Pop Culture DVD Game.

16. Jenga is a Swahili word that means "to build."

17. John Lloyd Wright, son of Frank Lloyd Wright, developed Lincoln Logs in 1916. John got the idea for the toy while traveling with his father in Tokyo.

18. The first board game was produced in 1843. It was called the Mansion of Happiness and it was made in Salem, Massachusetts. In this game, good deeds helped players move forward to the finish, while bad deeds caused them to move backward.

19. Parcheesi originated in India around 1570. The American version became popular in the 1860s.

20. Americans spend about $10.5 billion on video games annually. That's the same amount as shoppers spend on dolls, action figures, board games, arts and crafts, and sports toys combined.

21. The astronauts carried Silly Putty in special sterling silver eggs to play with in their spare time, and to hold their tools down while weightless.

22. Barbie's full name in Barbara Millicent Roberts. She is from Willows, Wisconsin, and attended Willows High School.

23. Empty aluminum pie plates from the Frisbee Baking Company were often used as flying discs once New England college students ate the pies.

24. Link is the hero in *The Legend of Zelda*. The original game debuted in 1987, and more than 13 versions of the game have been released since.

25. 43,252,003,274,489,856,000 is the number of color combinations possible on the Rubik's Cube. There are nine squares on each of the six sides, and each side is a different color.

26. The inside of an Etch-A-Sketch is filled with plastic beads and aluminum powder which allows users to draw.

27. A total of $15,140 is included in each Monopoly game. Each year, the manufacturers of the game print twice as much money as the U.S. Mint.

28. More than 1.5 billion Hot Wheels cars have been produced in the last four decades. That's more than the United States' top three carmakers combined.

29. Six 8-stud LEGO bricks of the same color can be combined 102,981,500 ways. Three 8-stud bricks of the same color can fit together in 1,060 ways. Two 8-stud same-colored bricks can be put together in 24 ways.

30. Two out of three American boys own a G.I. Joe action figure. Boys age 5 to 10 own approximately 10 G.I. Joes each.

31. Twister was originally called Pretzel, but when the inventor went to get a patent for the game, he found that the name was already patented.

32. More than 40 million Candy Land games have been sold in the United States. In fact, it's the top-selling game for preschoolers.

33. A brick is not one of the weapons included in Clue. The game's weapons include a candlestick, lead pipe, wrench, rope, revolver, and knife.

34. There are 28 possible missions in RISK, broken into seven types. The game, which debuted in 1959, is made up of 42 different territories which existed about 200 years ago.

35. The Magic 8 Ball does not use the answer "I Have No Idea." The fortune-telling toy has been helping people answer questions since 1946.

36. You need to win eight badges before you can enter Hoenn Pokémon League.

37. There is only one police officer career tile in the game. This is because every time a player spins a 10, the police officer gets $5,000.

38. Super Mario Bros. is the bestselling video game of all time, with more than 40 million sold since it was released in 1985.

39. Some 100,000 View Masters and six million picture reels were purchased by the government for military training during World War II.

40. Squeaker the Mouse was not an original Beanie Baby. The first nine included Cubbie the Bear, Chocolate the Moose, Spot the Dog, Flash the Dolphin, Legs the Frog, Patti the Platypus, Pinchers the Lobster, Splash the Whale, and Squealer the Pig.

41. Checkers was a favorite game among pharaohs in ancient Egypt and was often included in the tomb with the rulers' favorite possessions after death.

42. *Quartzy* is the highest-scoring word in Scrabble and is worth 164 points.

INDEX

PHOTO CREDITS

FOOD background: ©Photos.com; page 5, ©stock.xchng; page 6: ©stock.xchng, ©Dreamstime.com, ©Centers for Disease Control, ©Luiz Baltar/stock.xchng; page 7: ©Tom McNemar/Dreamstime.com, © Linnell Esler/stock.xchng, ©stock.xchng; page 8: ©stock.xchng, ©Artville; page 9: ©Photos.com, ©Raymond Kasprzak/Dreamstime.com; page 10: ©Photodisc, ©Fotosearch/Food Collection; page 11: ©Artville, ©Helmut Gevert/stock.xchng; page 12: Georgian Bay Associates, ©Photos.com, ©Julian Rovagnati/iStockphoto; page 13 and cover: ©Monika Adamczyk/Dreamstime.com, ©Kevin Gryczan/ iStockphoto, ©Colin Stitt/Dreamstime.com; page 14: ©iStockphoto, Georgian Bay Associates, ©Audrey Johnson/stock.xchng; page 15: ©Photos.com, ©Smiley Joanne iStockphoto; page 16: ©Photos.com, ©Sander Van de Wijngaert/Dreamstime.com; page 17 and cover: ©Paul Fairbrother/Dreamstime.com, ©Dragan Sasic/stock.xchng

SPORTS background: ©Alan Croswaithe/Dreamstime.com; page 18: ©Comstock, ©Photodisc; page 19: Photos.com, ©Photodisc; page 20: ©Photodisc, ©Toru Komiya/stock.xchng, ©Jozsef Szasz-Fabian/Dreamstime.com; page 21: ©Comstock, ©Photodisc; page 22: ©Comstock, ©Mario Alberto Magallanes Trejo/stock.xchng; page 23: ©Comstock, ©Philippe Wojazer/Reuters/Landov, ©Gary Lewis/Dreamstime.com; page 24: ©Connie Larsen/Dreamstime.com, ©Photodisc; page 25: ©Ezio Petersen/UPI/Landov, ©Dreamstime.com; page 26: ©Dreamstime.com, ©Comstock; page 27 and cover: ©Comstock, ©Photodisc; page 28: ©Dreamstime.com; page 29: ©Photodisc, ©Suzanne Tucker/iStockphoto; page 29: ©Comstock, ©Photodisc; page 31: ©Beth Van Trees/Dreamstime.com

ANIMALS background: ©Photos.com; page 33 and cover: ©Photos.com, ©Michael Shake/ Dreamstime.com; pages 34: ©Rob C. Nunnington; Gallo Images/Corbis, ©Neerav Bhatt/stock.xchng; page 35: ©Tony Campbell/iStockphoto, Photos.com; page 36 and cover: ©Photos.com, ©Paulo Ribas Jr./stock.xchng; page 37: © Paul Topp/iStockphoto; ©Brad Smith; page 38: ©Photos.com, ©Peter Caulfield/stock.xchng; page 39: Photos.com, ©Metaphotos; page 40: ©Michael Chen/iStockphoto, ©Vaida Petreikene/Dreamstime.com, ©Jake Williamson/stock.xchng; page 41: ©Photos.com, ©Matt Ragen/Dreamstime.com; page 42 and cover: ©Bruce Amos/Dreamstime.com; page 43: ©Photos.com; page 44: ©Kasia Petlak/stock.xchng, ©Bob Smith/stock.xchng; page 45: ©Photos.com

ENTERTAINMENT background: ©Dreamstime.com; page 46: ©Photos.com, ©MTV/ Photofest, ©20th Century Fox/Photofest; page 47: ©Walt Disney Pictures/Photofest, ©ABC/Photofest; page 48: ©Dreamstime.com; page 49: ©Tom Schmucker/Dreamstime.com, ©Lise Gagne/iStockphoto; page 50: ©Fox/Photofest, ©Peter Mountain/Warner Bros./Photofest; page 51: ©Walt Disney Pictures / Photofest, ©Nikki Nelson/WENN/Landov; page 52: ©Dreamstime.com, ©Toby Melville/Reuters/Landov; page 53: ©Buena Vista Pictures/Photofest; ©Associated Press; page 54: ©DreamWorks SKG/ZUMA/ Corbis, ©Matt Dunham/Reuters/Landov; page 55: ©The WB/Photofest, ©John Dunn/Associated Press, ©Michelle Preast/iStockphoto; page 56: ©Photofest, ©Scott Rothstein/Dreamstime.com; page 57: ©Nickelodeon/Photofest, ©20th Century Fox/Photofest; page 58: ©Walt Disney Pictures/Photofest, ©CBS/Landov; page 59: © Phil McCarten/Reuters/Corbis

HUMAN BODY background: ©Matt Gaston/Dreamstime.com; page 60 and cover: ©Sebastian Kaulitzki/Dreamstime.com, stock.xchng; page 61: ©Dreamstime.com, ©Peter Galbraith/Dreamstime. com, ©Photos.com; page 62: ©Mehmet Alci/Dreamstime.com, ©Dreamstime.com; page 63: ©Max Delson/iStockphoto; page 64: ©Courtnee Mulroy/Dreamstime.com; page 65: ©Scott Rothstein/ Dreamstime.com; page 66: Photos.com, ©Andrea Danti/Dreamstime.com, ©Dreamstime.com; page 87: ©Linda Bucklin/Dreamstime.com; page 68: ©Photos.com; page 69: ©Photos.com, ©Sebastian Kaulitzki/ Dreamstime.com; page 70: ©Photos.com; page 71: ©Photos.com, ©Olga Vasilkova/Dreamstime.com; page 72: ©Mandy Godbehear/Dreamstime.com, ©Danijel Micka/Dreamstime.com, ©Photodisc; page 73: ©Flavia Bottazzini/Dreamstime.com, ©Melissa King/Dreamstime.com; ©Photos.com

PHOTO CREDITS

STATISTICS background: ©Alex Puentes/Dreamstime.com; page 74: ©Photos.com, ©Jerry Horn/Dreamstime.com; page 75: ©Photos.com; page 76: ©Dreamstime.com, ©Chee-onn Leon/Dreamstime.com; page 77: Georgian Bay Associates; page 78: ©Photos.com, ©Rob Marmion/Dreamstime.com; page 79: ©Scott Kelsey/Dreamstime.com, ©David Simmonds/stock.xchng; page 80: ©Photos.com; page 81: ©Photos.com; page 82: © Hermann Danzmayr/Dreamstime.com, ©Photos.com; page 83: ©Photos.com, ©Tracy Hebden/Dreamstime.com; page 84: ©Daniel Sroga/Dreamstime.com, ©Photos.com; page 85: ©Steven Robertson/iStockphoto, ©Photos.com; page 86: ©Dreamstime.com

SCIENCE page 89: ©Jack Schiffer/Dreamstime.com, ©stock.xchng; page 88: ©Goce Ristesk/Dreamstime.com, ©National Aeronautics and Space Administration, © Mark Rasmussen/iStockphoto; page 89: ©Photos.com; page 90: ©Dreamstime.com, ©Denis Pepin/Dreamstime.com, ©Photos.com; page 91: © NASA/JPL-Caltech, ©Photos.com; page 92 and cover: ©Photos.com; page 93: © Alexandru Popescu/Dreamstime.com; page 94: ©Photos.com; page 95: ©Dreamstime.com; page 96: ©Photos.com; page 97: ©Vladimir Pomortsev/Dreamstime.com; page 98: ©Photos.com; page 99: ©Photos.com; page 100 and cover: ©Photos.com; page 101: ©Tomislav Stajduhar/Dreamstime.com; ©Photos.com;

WORLD background: ©Corbis; page 102: ©Jason Maehl/Dreamstime.com; page 103: ©Photos.com, ©Carsten Erler/Dreamstime.com; page 104: ©Dreamstime.com, ©Ryszard Laskowski/Dreamstime.com; page 105: ©Banana Stock, ©Darko Novakovic/Dreamstime.com; page 106: ©Dreamstime.com; page 107: ©Dreamstime.com, ©Robert Magorien/Dreamstime.com; page 108: Tamer Yazici/Dreamstime.com, ©Photos.com, ©Zbigniew Majerczyk/iStockphoto; page 109: ©Photos.com, ©stock.xchng; page 110: ©Christopher Ewing/Dreamstime.com; page 111 and cover: Antonio Petrone/Dreamstime.com, JoAnn Snover/Dreamstime.com; page 112: ©James Steidl/Dreamstime.com, ©Dreamstime.com, ©Photos.com; page 113: ©Max Dimyadi/Dreamstime.com, ©John Blanton/Dreamstime.com, ©Stephen Coburn/Dreamstime.com; page 114: ©Anita Patterson Peppers/Dreamstime.com, ©Photos.com, ©Christine Balderas/iStockphoto; page 115: ©stock.xchng

TOYS background: ©Photos.com; page 116: Georgian Bay Associates; page 117: Georgian Bay Associates, ©Lucía Pizarro Coma/stock.xchng; page 118: ©Mark Csabai/stock.xchng, Georgian Bay Associates; ©J. Andersen/stock.xchang; page 119: ©Scott Rothstein/Dreamstime.com, ©Lucía Pizarro Coma/stock.xchng; page 120: ©Tom Hemeryk/stock.xchng, Georgian Bay Associates; page 121: ©Robert Horvath/stock.xchng; page 122: ©Martina Berg/Dreamstime.com, ©Dreamstime.com; page 123: Georgian Bay Associates; page 124 and cover: ©Jeff Prieb/stock.xchng, ©Miguel Angel Salinas/Dreamstime.com, ©John Siebert/stock.xchng; page 125: ©Per-Åke Byström/stock.xchng, ©Daniel Wildman/stock.xchng, Georgian Bay Associates; page 126: Georgian Bay Associates; page 127: ©Thorsten Epping/stock.xchng, Georgian Bay Associates; page 128: Georgian Bay Associates; page 129: Georgian Bay Associates, ©Wh Chow/Dreamstime.com